Teach® Yourself

Marx – The Key Ideas

Gill Hands

D1268125

For UK order enquiries: please contact
Bookpoint Ltd, 130 Milton Park, Abingdon, Oxon, OX14 4SB.
Telephone: +44 (0) 1235 827720. Fax: +44 (0) 1235 400454.
Lines are open 09.00–17.00, Monday to Saturday, with a 24-hour
message answering service. Details about our titles and how to
order are available at www.teachyourself.co.uk

Long renowned as the authoritative source for self-guided
learning – with more than 50 million copies sold worldwide –
the **Teach Yourself** series includes over 500 titles in the fields of
languages, crafts, hobbies, business, computing and education.

British Library Cataloguing in Publication Data:
a catalogue record for this title is available from the British Library.

Library of Congress Catalog Card Number: on file.

First published in UK 2007 by Hodder Education, 338 Euston
Road, London, NW1 3BH.

First published in US 2007 by The McGraw-Hill Companies, Inc.

This edition published 2010.

Previously published as *Teach Yourself Marx*

The **Teach Yourself** name is a registered trade mark of
Hodder Headline.

Copyright © 2007, 2010 Gill Hands

Typeset by MPS Limited, A Macmillan Company.

Printed in Great Britain for Hodder Education, a division of
Hodder Headline, an Hachette Livre UK Company,
338 Euston Road, London, NW1 3BH, by Cox & Wyman Ltd,
Reading, Berkshire.

The publisher has used its best endeavours to ensure that the URLs
for external websites referred to in this book are correct and active
at the time of going to press. However, the publisher and the
author have no responsibility for the websites and can make no
guarantee that a site will remain live or that the content will remain
relevant, decent or appropriate.

Hodder Headline's policy is to use papers that are natural,
renewable and recyclable products and made from wood grown
in sustainable forests. The logging and manufacturing processes
are expected to conform to the environmental regulations of the
country of origin.

Impression number	10 9 8 7 6 5 4 3 2 1
Year	2010 2009 2008 2007

Contents

To my family and friends.

Also, many thanks to the illustrator for his brilliant cartoons.

Meet the author

Welcome to *Marx – The Key Ideas*!

I was born in Wales but have lived most of my life in Northern England. I have always been interested in all aspects of social history, including legend and folklore. After training as a teacher of English and History, specialising in the Victorian Era, I worked in Adult Training where I began teaching adults with disabilities and many adults who had missed out on formal education for various reasons. I was also instrumental in setting up three women's groups and a small press to give women in rural areas a voice. It was from working with these varied people that I acquired the skill of breaking complex subjects down into easier steps and clarifying difficult concepts. I have worked as a freelance writer for many years, writing Beginner's Guides to Marx and Darwin, as well as numerous newspaper and magazine articles, poetry and fiction. Like Marx, I believe that education is one of the first steps in the liberation of the individual.

Gill Hands, 2010

Only got a minute?

Karl Marx was born in Germany in 1818 at a time when Europe was going through great social changes as a result of industrialization and revolution. After studying philosophy he moved to Paris where he met Friedrich Engels and together they wrote *The Communist Manifesto* on behalf of the Communist League. Marx was then exiled from Paris and moved to London where he spent many years writing his masterwork *Das Kapital*.

Marx saw that the society around him was an unjust one where the workers, (proletariat) were exploited by the capitalist classes, (bourgeoisie). Marx believed that these two opposing groups made society unstable and this would inevitably lead to revolution. He proposed that after the revolution a fairer communist society would be set up, industry and money would be centralized and class distinctions would be abolished.

Marx died in 1883 but his ideas lived on and led to world changes. In 1917, after a revolution, Russia became the first communist state in the world and during the twentieth century many other countries followed. The communist societies that resulted were often a long way from Marx's ideal and eventually communism failed in many countries.

Although Marx's ideas have gone in and out of fashion they are still important today, for he was one of the first people to look at the exploitation and alienation caused by capitalist, consumer-led society. There has been a resurgence of interest in his predictions for the economy due to the global recession that began in 2007.

5 Only got five minutes?

Karl Marx was born in Germany in 1818 during a time at a time when Europe was going through great social changes as a result of industrialization and revolution. He was brought up in a conventional middle class family, and it was assumed that he would follow his father's profession, that of a small town lawyer. Marx initially studied law at university but contact with radicals led him to study philosophy instead. After university he concentrated on journalism and his articles on the plight of peasants soon put him in disfavour with the authorities. A short spell in Paris meant that he mixed with radicals and revolutionaries; it was here that he joined the Communist League and met with Friedrich Engels, his lifelong friend and co-writer. They wrote *The Communist Manifesto* in 1847.

Marx married his childhood sweetheart and had a large family. He was exiled from Paris and the family ended up living in London, where Marx was involved with International Workingman's Association. He wrote *Das Kapital*, an attempt to make a scientific study of politics, economics and capitalism. He lived in poverty for a great deal of his time in London and was financially supported by Engels. *Das Kapital* was not received well in Marx's lifetime and he died in some obscurity in 1883, but after his death the chain of ideas he had begun was to cause revolution and change society.

Philosophy

Marx was both a philosopher and an economist but he believed philosophy was not enough to change the world. His main contribution to the development of philosophy was historical materialism, a way of studying the relationship between the world of ideas and the material world. His study of philosophy and history led him to believe that society developed through a series of contradictions or dialects.

Economy and Society

Marx saw that society had developed into a capitalist one, focused on the production of commodities and that human labour power had itself become a commodity. This was exploited by the capitalists to gain profit. The capitalists (Bourgeoisie) were those who were rich enough to own factories and machinery and the workers (Proletariat) had to sell their labour power in order to live.

Marx believed capitalism led to fetishism (a kind of worship) of money, capital and commodities and this alienated people. This is because consumers do not see the relationship between a product that they buy and the work that has gone into making it.

Class struggle and revolution

Marx believed that capitalism had divided society into two opposing camps, the Bourgeoisie and the Proletariat. He thought people were influenced by ideology, i.e. the prevailing perceptions of a society, to believe that the society they lived in was a fair one that could not be changed; everyone had their place and things had always been that way. He believed that once the Proletariat became educated and realised they were being exploited then they would begin a revolution.

Further Marxist thought

Marx believed that all the injustices in society could only be remedied by the communist society that would be set up as the result of the inevitable revolution. The means of production would be centralised, private property would be abolished and money would cease to exist. Religion would also be abolished as Marx saw it as the *opium of the people*, something that gave an illusory support to those suffering from alienation and poverty.

How Marxism changed the world

After Marx's death Engels continued with his work and Marx's ideas began to spread around the world. Russia became the first communist state in the world after a revolution in 1917 and remained in isolation until Mao Zedong declared the People's Republic of China in 1949. Other countries followed suit, mainly in the developing world. The communist societies that resulted from these revolutions were often a long way from the ideals of Marx, and communism failed in many countries largely because of economic problems.

Marxism after Marx

Numerous schools of Marxism flourished in the twentieth century and academics hotly debated the 'true' meaning of Marx's legacy. There has been a great deal of debate about the relevance of Marx in the 21st century and Marx has gone in and out of fashion in academic circles. Post-modern theorists such as Jean Baudrillard have argued that Marx's economic theories do not take the world of the mass media and modern consumerism into account and those who follow the philosophy of Jean-Francois Lyotard think that huge theories of everything and grand narratives, like those Marx described in *Das Kapital,* are flawed. There was a resurgence of interest in Marx's predictions for the economy after the start of the world economic crisis that began in 2007. There is also interest in his ideas on consumerism by those in the green movement who see capitalism as the main enemy of the environment.

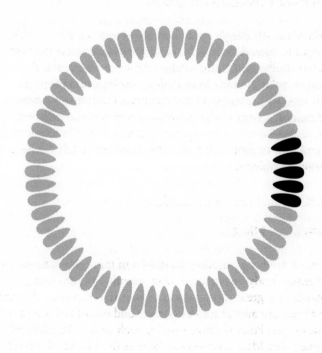

10 Only got ten minutes?

Karl Marx was born in Germany in 1818 when the Industrial Revolution and the French Revolution were changing the face of Europe. It was while he was at university that Marx developed an interest in the philosophy of Georg Hegel and the theory of the dialectic, the idea that change comes about as a result of conflict between two opposing movements. After university Marx moved to Paris and began collaborating with Friedrich Engels, who was to become his lifelong friend and co-writer. They wrote *The Communist Manifesto* together in 1847.

Marx and his family lived in London, and Marx became involved with the International Workingmen's Association. This was founded in 1864, when trade unionists from many countries decided it would be in their interests to band together. Marx lived in poverty for a great deal of his time in London and was financially supported by Engels. Marx wrote *Das Kapital*, an attempt to make a scientific study of politics, economics and capitalism. It was not received well in Marx's lifetime, however after his death 1883 the chain of ideas he had begun was to eventually cause revolution and change society.

Philosophy

Marx was both a philosopher and an economist and his main contribution to the development of philosophy was historical materialism, a way of studying the relationship between the world of ideas and the material world.

Marx studied philosophy at Berlin University and became interested in the works of the ancient Greek philosophers Democritus and Epicurus. Marx also studied the philosophers Georg Wilhelm Friedrich Hegel and Ludwig Andreas Feuerbach. Both Hegel and Feuerbach believed that people became alienated because they were separate from God but Marx realized that it was money that alienated people in society.

Economy

Marx explained his economic theory in his works *Das Kapital*, *Wage-labour and Capital,* and *Value, Price and Profit*. He saw that since the Industrial Revolution society had focused on the production of commodities and that human labour power had itself become a commodity.

Marx saw that workers are exploited in an industrialized society but the exploitation is hidden. It is only in an industrialized capitalist economy that costly machinery and factories, the means of production, are needed before products can be made. In this way the capitalists or bourgeoisie, i.e. those who were rich enough to own the means of production, came to be the new ruling class. As more and more people left the land to work in factories their labour power became a commodity that could be bought and sold. Marx believed workers were exploited because factory owners could make a profit from their workers and then invest it to make more profit. This is what Marx called the theory of surplus value.

Marx believed that this drive to make profits would push wages lower and lower and this was one of the factors that would eventually lead to global economic crisis; high wages reduce the profit of the capitalist, but low wages mean that workers are unable to buy enough goods and services to keep the economy viable. Because capitalists are in competition with each other and there is no system of regulation of who produces what, there is a danger of over-production; prices fall and the economy becomes stagnant or depressed. Factory owners are also interdependent because no producer can meet all of his own needs from the products of his own factory so he has to sell them as commodities in order to buy other commodities. Marx saw these factors as inherent instabilities in the capitalist system and predicted a series of booms and periodic depressions. His solution, under a communist government, was the centralization of production and of the economy.

Society

Marx saw how the rapid spread of capitalism around the world had led to colonialism, where one country exploited another for profit. Marx saw the globalization of world markets as inevitable, because as profits fell in home markets factory owners would try and exploit new markets overseas. It was this exploitation that is believed to be a contribution to the formation of the developing world.

Marx thought that work was necessary to the human condition, but he believed the factory system had distorted natural relations between people, placing them in competition with each other. He also thought that they were not in 'right relation' to the goods that they produced and this led to alienation of people in society. Marx believed capitalism led to fetishism (a kind of worship) of money, capital and commodities and this was part of the process of alienation. This is because consumers do not see the relationship between a product that they buy and the work that has gone into making it. This is linked to exploitation which is not apparent to those in the society

Class struggle and revolution

Marx believed capitalism had divided society into two opposing camps, the bourgeoisie and the proletariat.

The bourgeoisie were the class of capitalists, who owned the means of production and employed wage labourers. The proletariat were the workers, who had no means of production of their own and were reduced to selling their labour.

Although workers were exploited they accepted the status quo because they did not understand that they were being exploited. Marx believed the only way of changing this was to begin a revolutionary workers party to educate working people. This was one of the reasons that he became involved with the Communist League and wrote *The Communist Manifesto*. He thought that when the proletariat had become a class 'for itself' then revolution would follow.

Further Marxist thought

In a communist society private property would be abolished, class distinctions would disappear, and eventually society would become a self-governing community. Work would still exist but there would be no alienation or exploitation.

Although *The Communist Manifesto* puts forward some ways in which a communist society might be run there is not much detail in any of Marx's writings. A lot of what we know about this subject is taken from the work of Engels, in particular *The Principles of Communism*, written in 1847. Engels proposed that banks and industry would be nationalized, there would be free education, slums would be demolished to make way for communal housing, private property would be abolished and eventually money would cease to exist.

How Marxism changed the world

After Marx's death in 1883, Engels continued with his work. With the help of Eleanor Marx, Marx's youngest daughter, he started to make the later volumes of *Das Kapital* fit for publication. The ideas of Marx led to Russia becoming the first communist country in the world in 1917. The civil war that followed meant that the economy was left in ruins and a true communist state did not emerge. Instead the Soviet Union became a virtual dictatorship under the leadership of Josef Stalin.

Marxism after Marx

Numerous schools of Marxism flourished in the twentieth century during which academics hotly debated the 'true' meaning of Marx's legacy. Classical Marxism is the theory of Marxism that Marx and Engels developed. It is based on what Marx said or wrote. Lenin and Stalin in the Soviet Union, and Mao Zedong in China, developed their own forms of Marxism as they struggled to make communism work. Marx's ideas were further developed by thinkers such as the Italian communist, Antonio Gramsci, who brought in the theory of hegemony – a development of Marx's theory of ideology.

The philosophers of the Frankfurt School developed a form of Marxism sometimes know as Western Marxism. They looked at critiquing society as a whole in order to bring about desired changes.

There has been a great deal of debate about the relevance of Marx in the twenty-first century and Marx has gone in and out of fashion in academic circles. Post-modern theorists, such as Jean Baudrillard, argued that Marx's economic theories do not take mass media and modern consumerism into account; and those who follow the philosophy of Jean-Francois Lyotard think that 'grand narratives' like those Marx described in *Das Kapital*, are flawed. There was a resurgence of interest in Marx's predictions for the economy after the start of the world economic crisis that began in 2007. There is also interest in his ideas on consumerism by those in the green movement who see capitalism as the main enemy of the environment.

Introduction

Karl Marx is considered to be one of the greatest thinkers of the last thousand years. Born in Germany in 1818, he was a great philosopher, historian, economist and social theorist. What I find fascinating is that he was not a specialist in any of these areas of expertise, but his writing led to revolution and to a total change in the political structure of the world.

Marx lived during a time of great social and industrial change in Europe and this book explains the historical context of his writings, how they led to revolution after his death and the rise and fall of communist states. I am interested in the way society, morals and manners change through the ages. Marx was interested in many of the same factors, and his analysis of ideology (the assumptions each society makes about the nature of the world), seems obvious to us today. At the time it was a radical idea to say that people can only think in the way that their language and the concepts handed down to them allow.

Marx became almost a god to those living under communism; I find this ironic as Marx believed that 'religion is the opium of the people.' He became a well known figurehead for the Communist world and subject to so much propaganda that details about his life and work are often misunderstood. He is known as the 'father of communism,' although he did not invent this title. The word 'communist' came into the English language in 1840, coined by Goodwyn Barmby the founder of the London Communist Propaganda Society. He derived it from the French word 'commune', a description of the social structure that emerged after the French Revolution. However such is the iconic power of Marx that he will always be identified with the word in everybody's minds. It is also the case that many of his sayings have become well known but are often misquoted or misunderstood. People often talk of the 'bourgeoisie' or the 'proletariat' without knowing exactly what the terms mean. This book is an introduction to his thought and so all terms and jargon are explained in the text.

Despite being an iconic figure Marx was only human, with human weaknesses and prejudices. He had a towering intellect and a volatile and forceful personality, often clashing with other thinkers of his day, but he was a loving family man and father to his children. They lived in poverty for a great deal of their lives because he continued to write about and support a cause he believed in. He wrote vividly about the horrors of the factory system, yet he depended heavily on an industrialist, Friedrich Engels, for financial support in order to write what is considered to be his great masterwork. This analysis of class structure and the industrial capitalist system took many years of his life and took a toll on his health.

Marx did not live in a vacuum, he was influenced greatly by the German philosophers Georg Wilhelm Friedrich Hegel and Ludwig Feuerbach; by British political economists Adam Smith and David Ricardo; and by French socialists including Charles Fourier, Henri de Saint-Simon, Pierre-Joseph Proudhon and Louis Blanc. Their influence on him is explained in detail in the chapter on philosophy which shows the development of his own thought processes into a Marxist philosophy.

Marx challenged the received wisdom of his day and prompted questions about the nature of society and class structure. He looked for patterns of development in the history of mankind and used these to understand and comment on the capitalist system. He documented the rise of the Industrial Revolution and the power of capitalist society. He saw that modern industry had a great potential for improving lives but instead it crushed and impoverished people because it was a tool of a capitalist system that he was deeply critical of. He believed the capitalist system exploited and alienated those who lived under it, so that money came to rule the lives of both rich and poor. He was one of the first writers to examine the beginnings of the consumer-led society that we now live in and he predicted it would spread around the world.

His view of the world was one of class struggle, where one dominant class had come to oppress another. He believed that this could not last and it would lead to an inevitable world-wide revolution. This would be followed by the setting up of societies of equals under communism. In the twentieth century this seemed to be a real possibility as more and more countries came under communist rule, but true communism as Marx envisaged it, did not follow and many communist states had collapsed by the end of the century.

The fall of communist regimes in many countries has led to doubts about Marx's relevance in the twenty-first century. He predicted world-wide revolution, which hasn't happened and these facts have led to a great discussion over the validity of his theories. Were they only applicable to the time in which he was writing, or are they still applicable? Might a revolution still be a possibility? Did the world financial crisis that began in 2007 show that he was right about the inherent instability of the capitalist system? There are no easy answers to these questions but the book presents many of the key facts and ideas so that the reader is invited to make up his or her own mind.

There are numerous books about Marx on the market that assume the reader already has an understanding of economics and philosophy. Many books are written by academics for other academics, who already know what Marx wrote and wish to discuss the finer points of his ideas in detail. This book aims to give a background to his life and times, an understanding of the key areas of Marx's thought and to show how his ideas have affected the world we live in today. It makes more sense if read in order from cover to cover as it follows the development of his thought, although chapters can be read in isolation.

Marx was a prolific writer and there is no way that a book introducing his theories can cover all the points that he made, or attempt to analyse all the arguments for and against what he believed. At the end of the book there is a reading list for those who want a deeper understanding of what Marx said and further insight into the philosophical, political and academic arguments that his work has inspired over the last century.

1

Marx's early life

In this chapter you will learn:
- *about Marx's personal life and character*
- *the background to the society in which he lived*
- *key facts about his early life and career*
- *about his work on* **The Communist Manifesto**
- *why he became an exile.*

Europe at the time of Marx

Karl Marx was born on 5 May 1818, during a time of rapid social change throughout Europe. There were two main forces for this change. The first was the **Industrial Revolution** that had started in Britain. This led to the growth of the factory system throughout Europe and to an increase in the size and number of cities.
The invention of the steam engine and the spread of the factory system meant that people were beginning to live in a completely different way to their ancestors. In the past, people had lived and worked in closely knit communities and worked in traditional agriculture or as craftsmen. They now began flocking from rural areas into the huge new cities that were beginning to spring up all over Europe.

Agricultural reforms and machinery had increased the efficiency of farms and led to unemployment in rural areas. In addition, landowners took over common rights and grazing areas that had once belonged to everyone under the feudal system. This also increased rural poverty.

The new towns and cities were soon flooded with destitute farmers, craftsmen and their families who were desperate for work under any circumstance. They mainly worked long hours for subsistence wages in factories and mines that were completely unregulated. Even young children worked for hours with unguarded and dangerous machinery. These unfortunate people lived in appalling conditions: squashed into slum housing with inadequate sanitation, poor food and no clean drinking water. Disease was rife and mortality rates were high.

Secondly, the **French Revolution** of 1789 and the Napoleonic wars (1799–1815) had led to the downfall of the monarchy and the abolition of feudalism throughout much of Europe. The feudal system was a society where the power of the ruling class, or aristocracy, rested on its control of farmable lands or fiefs. The way these societies worked varied from country to country, but in general the lands were divided out among vassals (free men), who managed them in return for military service on behalf of the aristocracy. The land was then farmed by serfs or peasants, who were not free. Marx believed that this led to a class society based upon the **exploitation** of the peasants who farmed the lands. His views on this are discussed later in the book.

Marx's birthplace, Trier in the Rhineland, was then part of Prussia, in central Europe. Prussia was a large semi-feudal empire that covered what is known today as Germany and parts of what are now Poland and Sweden. Prussia had been invaded on several occasions by the French and Trier had been part of Napoleon's Confederation of the Rhine. When Napoleon was eventually defeated and exiled in 1815, Prussia returned to being a set of kingdoms and principalities ruled by hereditary monarchies. At the end of the Napoleonic wars, state boundaries were redefined and an agreement was drawn up between Prussia, Russia and

Austria; this was known as the 'Holy Alliance'. It was an attempt by the ruling classes to preserve the social order; the aristocracy and landowners were determined to hang on to power now they had regained it.

Prussia was really a very loose patchwork of scattered countries, so it had always had a large army to keep order and had a government-controlled **economy.** Revolutions were sweeping through most of Europe and fear of these changes led to the Prussian state becoming overly bureaucratic, backward-looking and resistant to trade and industry. The police were particularly powerful as landowners were fearful of the democratic ideals that had led to the French Revolution. There was a deep suspicion of any new ideas, especially those that were seen to be liberal. Many free thinkers, including artists, writers and poets, moved to Paris or Switzerland to escape from this oppressive regime. Most liberal thinkers in Prussia wanted to see a united German state with a democratic constitution. In contrast the conservatives of the time wanted to keep Germany as separate countries within the Prussian Empire.

Marx's father, Heinrich Marx, was a lawyer. He was Jewish and came from a family that had several rabbis in its history, but he had registered as a Protestant Christian when laws were passed preventing Jews from holding public positions. Marx's mother, Henriette, was a Dutch Jew who also came from a family that included a long line of rabbis. Marx himself did not hold any strong religious beliefs and ended his life as an atheist, but the strong anti-Jewish feeling in the Rhineland during his youth must have had some influence on him.

Although Prussia was a mainly agricultural country, the area of the Rhineland where Marx grew up was its most industrialized region. Marx's early life there meant that he observed rural life under threat, experienced repression of religious belief and understood the power of the State and private ownership, all at first hand. These formative experiences had a part in shaping his later philosophy.

The early life of Marx

Marx's upbringing was a middle-class one. Little is known of his very early life as he became somewhat estranged from his family in his later life. He came from a fairly large family with both brothers and sisters, but he was the oldest son and his brothers both died young.

His father was said to be a serious, well-educated man but not particularly imaginative. He wanted his children to fit in with the society around them and he tried to encourage them to be good members of the State and church. He was a bit of a social climber and became a member of the Casino Club, where in 1816 he met Baron von Westphalen, a senior government officer from an aristocratic family. The two families soon became friendly; Marx's older sister Sophie was a great friend of the Baron's daughter Jenny, and Karl was at school with Edgar, one of the Baron's sons.

Marx's mother was not formally educated but this was fairly normal for women at the time. She put all her energies into bringing up her family and was forever anxious about them, even when they had grown up and left home.

Young Karl was soon seen to be possessed of a strong and creative intelligence. He was fiercely independent, domineering and argumentative from a young age. His sisters told his daughter Eleanor that he used to force them to eat mud pies but they put up with it because he would tell them imaginative stories that they loved to listen to.

His intelligence soon caught the attention of their family friend Baron von Westphalen. The Baron was a very cultured and educated man, somewhat **radical** in his beliefs and fond of literature, including Shakespeare, who he liked to quote in the original English. The Baron became friendly with young Karl and encouraged him in his studies; they often took walks together and talked about Greek poetry. He lent many of his own books to the boy so that he could further his education and Marx dedicated his doctoral thesis to him in appreciation.

It is thought that Marx was privately educated until he joined the Trier High School in 1830 at the age of 13. His school records do not show flashes of any particular genius but he showed signs of independent thought and of not going along with the crowd in his refusal to talk to a new state-appointed headmaster who was given a position at the school.

The old headmaster was a man of fairly liberal ideas and this led to a police raid on the school in 1832: literature in support of free speech was found circulating there and one of the schoolboy ringleaders was expelled. The headmaster was put under surveillance and eventually the authorities employed a very conservative co-headmaster to keep an eye on things. Marx would not talk to this man at all, and was one of the few boys who did not visit him after he graduated from school, much to his father's embarrassment.

Although intellectually powerful, Marx never had a particularly strong constitution and was dogged by ill health for most of his life. He had a weak chest, which eventually led to him being found unfit for military service in 1836. His parents constantly fretted about his health when he went off to university in Bonn at the age of 17. They bombarded him with letters advising him not to study more than his health could bear, not to smoke, stay up late, drink too much wine and to keep his rooms and himself clean and hygienic. He never took much notice of their advice and for most of his life he lived in a disordered way, smoked and drank far too much, and spent long hours studying and writing.

University life

Marx attended Bonn University in the autumn of 1835 with the intention of studying law. He soon found that it was not to his taste and spent most of his year there in time-honoured student traditions: running up debts and drinking. His father's letters are full of complaint, accusing him of debauchery, lounging in a dressing gown with unkempt hair and of not taking his studies seriously enough. It is not surprising that he felt this way, for the student Marx was arrested and imprisoned overnight for drunken behaviour and rowdiness, was found with a pistol in his possession (strictly illegal, although he got off without charges when his father intervened), and was later wounded in a duel. The wound was above his left eye and left a lasting scar. As his opponent was a trained soldier he was lucky to get away so lightly.

Marx was a rather arresting figure with a shock of dark hair, piercing eyes and a rather large flourishing beard. His dark complexion led to the nickname of Moor, which he kept all through his life; it became a special family name for him that even his children used. Although his voice was not commanding (he had a slight lisp), his intellectual abilities and inventive way with words meant that he was often listened to and deferred to by older students. He found an outlet for his ideas in the Poetry Club, where political ideas as well as literature were discussed. This meant that he did not spend as much time on his studies as he should have and eventually his father insisted that he should stop his 'wild rampaging' and move to a place with a more rigorous academic atmosphere.

In the autumn of 1836 he entered the University of Berlin, again with the intention of studying law. Berlin was a much bigger place than Bonn and the university had the reputation of being seriously academic and a centre of radical thought in the form of the '**Young Hegelians**'. These were a group of academics, intellectuals and students who discussed and developed the ideas of the German philosopher **Georg Wilhelm Friedrich Hegel** (1770–1831).

Hegel had been the rector at the university and was almost an institution there. He was the nearest thing to an officially endorsed **philosopher** that existed, having been decorated by Fredrick William III for services to the Prussian Empire. Most of his followers received appointments or preferment in the universities, for even these were controlled by the State. Hegel's philosophy is rather complex and is discussed in more detail in Chapter 3, but basically he believed that society progressed by intellectual development or 'Reason' and that Reason could be identified with a God-like figure he called the 'Absolute'. Hegel asserted that the Absolute had developed throughout history, but it had come to consciousness of itself and culminated its development in the state of Prussia. There was no further progress for it to make as it had reached its ideal.

The Young Hegelians agreed to some extent that the State should be the embodiment of Reason but they interpreted the theories of Hegel in increasingly radical ways. They saw the Absolute not as a God-like figure but as humanity itself. For a reader in the twenty-first century this does not seem particularly shocking but at the time the Church was a very powerful force in society. To suggest that mankind might be at the centre of the universe and not some God or Absolute was very daring. It was much later, in November 1859, that Charles Darwin made his theory of evolution public in *The Origin of Species*, and Friedrich Nietzsche, who saw that scientific discoveries had led to Western society becoming more secular and thought this might lead to a nihilistic viewpoint of a world without meaning, didn't proclaim 'God is Dead' until 1882.

Insight

Charles Darwin's suggestion that mankind had evolved from apes caused more public outcry in its day than any work by Marx and it is still a contentious issue for some people with deeply held religious beliefs.

The Young Hegelians were a potentially powerful political force; many of them were atheists and liberals. They argued that the Prussian state was not the culmination of Reason and expression of the Absolute. They believed that things could be changed and Germany could become more democratic. This led to the authorities being increasingly worried about their activities and, as the Prussian state was well supplied with spies and informers, in addition to a large police force, they kept an eye on the activities of the Young Hegelians. Most of their activities were theoretical: they wrote about the problems, discussed them in bars and debated points of philosophy in great academic detail. They did not take action and this was one of the reasons that Marx finally lost patience with them. As he wrote later in his *Thesis on Feuerbach*, 'The philosophers have only interpreted the world in various ways; the point is to change it'.

When Marx first arrived at the university he did not think much of the philosophy of Hegel, in fact he disregarded it, for he was meant to be studying law (although he did not find his classes particularly interesting). He spent his first term writing rather a lot of romantic poetry to his childhood friend Jenny von Westphalen. She had grown into a beautiful, cultured and intelligent young woman and they had seen quite a lot of each other during the summer break and had become secretly engaged. Marx told his family about his love for her but it was kept a secret from Jenny's family for over a year. They were madly in love and wrote each other very romantic letters; Jenny affectionately called him her 'little wild boar'.

Although Baron von Westphalen was fond of Marx, the couple did not think that he would approve of the match as Marx was not from the kind of family that a young lady should consider marrying into. The von Westphalens belonged to a much higher social class than a lawyer's family. Also Jenny was four years older than Marx and officially engaged to a young army officer. She thought it best if they kept their love a secret until she had time to talk to her father.

As the academic year went on, Marx found he was becoming increasingly uninterested in the study of law, but he was not sure what he wanted to do with his life. He read voraciously and began his lifelong habit of taking notes on everything he read. He tried to write a philosophy of law and he wrote poetry, plays and a short comic novel but it seems that he suddenly realized in a flash that he would never be a 'real' poet or writer of the kind he wished to be. Eventually, he had a breakdown and was sent into the country by his doctor for a rest. It was there that he read Hegel and became a convert to the Hegelian point of view, something he had resisted for a long time.

From then on Marx became an active member of Hegelian societies in Berlin. He joined the Doctors' Club in 1837 – a group of young Hegelian intellectuals that included Bruno Bauer, a theology lecturer and Arnold Ruge, a radical philosopher.

His father disapproved of such radical ideas and was horrified, especially as he could see that his son was being drawn away from his law studies into the world of philosophy and intellectualism that he despised – 'the workshop of senseless and inexpedient erudition' was his description in a letter. This was the beginning of a major split between Marx and his family, for he never returned home to them in the holidays again and hardly ever replied to their letters. When his father died of tuberculosis later in that year he did not go to his funeral, claiming that he was too busy, although he always kept his father's photograph and it was finally buried with him.

Marx attended very few lectures in his three years at Berlin University and he put most of his energies into philosophy. He rather neglected his fiancée Jenny as he was spending a lot of time with free thinking, free drinking intellectuals and their friends, who had a more bohemian way of life than he had experienced in his middle-class, country-town upbringing.

Insight

A bohemian lifestyle was a life of artistic freedom that began to be described in the early nineteenth century. Many creative people often chose voluntary poverty and moved into the poorer quarters of cities as an escape from restrictive social codes, or because they held unconventional moral or anti-establishment views.

Marx even became temporarily romantically entangled with a famous poet, Bettina von Armin, who was old enough to be his mother. The liaison did not last for long, especially after he took her back home to meet his fiancée.

One of his closest friends at the time was Bruno Bauer, who later became one of his enemies. Marx had a habit of forming very close friendships throughout his life, but when his ideas moved on and his friends didn't he often ended up being totally antagonistic towards them, ridiculing them with very personal invectives, even though (and perhaps because) he had once shared the same ideas and believed in the same principles. He poured a lot of his energy into almost childish, involved attacks on people who had once been good friends.

Bauer was a theology lecturer and prominent in the Young Hegelians. He encouraged Marx to drop his law studies and concentrate on philosophy. He believed Marx would suit an academic life more than that of a small-town lawyer.

So Marx began work on his thesis, *The Difference Between the Democritean and Epicurean Philosophy*, hoping that this would allow him to earn a doctorate and enable him to lecture at Berlin University. It was ostensibly a discussion of ancient Greek philosophy but it was actually quite a radical piece of work for the times, as Marx argued that philosophy should be detached from religion and freed from all kinds of dogma.

Unfortunately, Marx chose a bad time to write on such a contentious subject as there was a radical change of policy at the university and a lot of Young Hegelians lost their jobs. Marx knew that his thesis would be marked by a very stuffy and reactionary lecturer who would probably fail him, so he sent it to the University of Jena which had a reputation of giving degrees quickly and easily. He earned his PhD in April 1841 and then spent most of the summer in Bonn philosophizing and getting drunk with Bruno Bauer. They got up to all sorts of pranks and jokes: galloping donkeys along the main street and writing a comic pamphlet in which they pretended they were shocked by the atheism of Hegel. This last joke backfired, as Bauer was dismissed from his university post and with him went any chance of Marx becoming a lecturer there.

Life as a journalist

Now that Marx had no chance of getting the academic post he had been hoping for he was uncertain of what to do next. His father's death had left him without any allowance and his mother, who he did not visit, had kept back his share of the family estate. He travelled about aimlessly for a few months before settling down to his first and only career. He had always written clearly and lucidly and so he began to publish some of his writing.

He began his journalistic career with a piece on censorship in the Young Hegelian journal *Deutsche Jarbrucker* in February 1842; the piece was brilliantly written but sadly and inevitably it was censored before publication. The journal was too radical for the times and it was closed down after a few months.

Marx then moved to Cologne and began work as a journalist on the *Rheinische Zeitung*, a liberal newspaper that had been founded in 1841 by a consortium of wealthy manufacturers and industrialists.

At that time, Cologne was a city at the forefront of the new technological and industrial advances brought on by the Industrial Revolution and it was the largest city in the Rhineland. It became a magnet for anyone who wished for a more democratic or unified Germany and who believed in freedom of the press and freedom of speech. The industrialists believed in progress and were willing to finance projects that would lead to advances in German society. They thought that the newspaper would be a good way of promoting their aims.

Adolf Rutenberg, the editor of *Rheinische Zeitung*, knew Marx very well. He had been a drinking companion in the Doctors' Club and he was also the brother-in-law of Bruno Bauer. Marx's assistant at the paper was Moses Hess, who soon became a good friend, although not unusually they were to fall out later.

Marx was soon writing hard-hitting articles, criticizing both the government and some of the liberals who opposed them in very uncomplimentary ways. His forceful nature meant that he became editor of the paper in October 1842. Once in charge he offended many of the people who had been writing for the paper previously, believing that some of their work was too frivolous. He fiercely criticized theories he felt were not thought out or argued properly.

He also came into conflict with the censor many times. Every paper in Prussia had to be checked over by a public censor before it was allowed to be published, and Marx delighted in baiting and annoying the censor with obscure references and word games. When the censor believed something was not suitable for publication (as he often did), Marx would spend long hours arguing with him. Marx used his formidable intellectual powers to persuade the censor to change his mind and he often worried that Marx would make him lose his job.

It was during his time at the paper that Marx realized his knowledge of social and economic matters was not very wide and was too theoretical. He began to study political economy seriously and to take a more practical and materialistic interest in the world around him. One of his most controversial pieces was written about the plight of peasants when a new law was brought out dealing with thefts of wood.

Under the old feudal system of government the peasants had the right to gather firewood in the forests. When the forests passed into private ownership the peasants had to pay for their wood and most of them could not afford to. The laws were so strictly absurd that people could even be fined for picking up a fallen twig. Marx did not hesitate to write a strongly worded article about this. He also wrote about the plight of wine growers in the Moselle region who had been badly affected by the imposition of tariffs and the importing of tariff-free wines. These were some of the earliest incidences of documentary reporting and it was at this time that Marx first began to think and write about matters of private property, economics, class struggle and State power.

The readership of the paper grew greatly under his editorship and it began to cause consternation in government circles. In January 1843, the paper and its editor were prosecuted for the article about the peasants' firewood and the paper was closed down by order of the government in Berlin. The closure of the paper was largely due to the intervention of Tsar Nicholas I of Russia, who had taken exception to an anti-Russian piece that had also appeared in the paper that January.

Although Marx was now out of a job again he was not unhappy about it, because he had begun to realize he was feeling restricted by government policies, censorship and the need to placate officials. He saw that Bauer and his other old friends at the Doctors' Club were intellectually isolated and too theoretical, spending far too much time on academic argument and the denunciation of religion. Marx wanted to do more. He wanted to be able to write freely and passionately about what he believed in. He knew that this would no longer be possible for him in Prussia and so in 1843 he moved to Paris.

Marx moved to Paris as a married man, for he had finally taken Jenny as his wife after a seven-year engagement. Baron von Westphalen had eventually given his approval of the match but had died before the wedding. The happy couple married in June 1843 at Kreuznach, a fashionable spa town. Jenny's half-brother

Ferdinand was head of the family and showed his disapproval by not attending, but her younger brother Edgar attended, as did her mother who gave them a large sum of cash to set up home with. This was soon gone as they spent it on having a good time during their honeymoon. They were also given a present of some old family silver that became very useful to them later in their marriage but possibly not in the way that Jenny's mother had intended – it was often in the pawn shop!

Even during his honeymoon Marx continued to write, working on the *Contribution to the Critique of Hegel's Philosophy of Right*. This was not published until 1927 but in it we can see that Marx hoped for radical political change in German society through democratic means. At that time he had not formulated any theories of workers' revolution.

Paris was the revolutionary capital of Europe with a large population of refugees including thousands of expatriate Germans. Dissidents were drawn in by the reputation of past revolutions, even though France was once again under the rule of a monarchy. It was here that Marx came into contact with communist and revolutionary sects, with numerous members from all walks of life including artisans and workers.

Marx had moved to Paris after persuasion from Arnold Ruge, his old friend from Berlin University. Ruge hoped that his family, Marx and Jenny and the German poet Heine and his wife, could live together in a communal way as a kind of experiment. Heine's wife would have nothing to do with it and the experiment failed after only two weeks because Ruge and his wife could not tolerate Marx's untidiness and his nocturnal writing. Marx and Jenny moved into their own apartment and their first child Jenny, also known as Jennychen, was born in May 1844.

Marx became editor of a new paper that Ruge had set up, *The German-French Annals*. Although this only ran for one issue because of censorship problems, it was an important part in the development of Marx's thought processes because it was the first time that he had written something that was directed more at the worker than the intellectual.

It was in Paris that Marx really came face to face with working-class people and it totally changed the way he thought about the possibilities of **communism**.

Insight

It is important to remember that communism existed as a development from the ideals of French revolution before Marx wrote about it, but Marx and Engels were the first to popularize the term as founding members of the Communist League.

As a student Marx wrote in theoretical and abstract terms; as a journalist he began writing about the practical problems of the poor and their struggle against private property but he was not really involved with them in any real sense. Finally, in Paris he began to meet with workers and to study political **economists,** such as Adam Smith. He began to think about society and the economy in materialist terms – real terms not abstract visions. He became convinced by the power of working men to change society during an uprising of Silesian weavers. This led to a huge argument with Ruge who wrote about the weavers' rebellion in very critical terms. It ended their friendship and Marx's connection with the Young Hegelians.

Marx met many revolutionaries and liberal thinkers in Paris and he became very friendly with the **anarchists** Pierre Joseph Proudhon and Mikhail Bakunin and with Heinrich Heine the German poet.

Insight

Anarchists advocate that the state does not need government. The rise in anarchy in the nineteenth century developed from the aftermath of the French Revolution. This led to the term anarchy being used to describe a state of political and social chaos, which is not intended in the original use of the word.

Although the Annals closed down they had a wide readership in Germany and among German exiles because Marx persuaded Heine to write some satirical socialist poems. Incidentally, Heine was one of the few friends that Marx did not later fall out with as he believed allowances should be made for poets. He told his daughter Eleanor that he did not believe poets should be judged by the standards that apply to other people, but he was also forever grateful because he believed Heine had saved the life of little Jennychen by plunging her into a cold bath when she had convulsions.

The new influences Marx found in Paris led him to write the *Economic and Philosophic Manuscripts* in 1844. They were not published until 1932 but in these we can see him grasping towards some of his later theories on the materialist view of history and the role of the worker in capitalism. These theories are discussed in detail later in this book.

Marx became reacquainted with **Friedrich Engels** (their paths had crossed very briefly during Marx's early journalistic career). Engels had a reputation as a radical journalist and young Hegelian and wanted to contribute to the Annals. He had written for the *Rheinische Zeitung* but at that time Marx had believed him to be too much of a theorist and distrusted his ideas. Since then Engels had gone to work in Manchester for his father's firm and he saw the terrible poverty in the city and the Industrial Revolution at first hand. He had become involved with the Chartist movement (an early form of trade unionism) and his association with a factory girl, Mary Burns, who became his mistress, meant that he visited slum areas that people from his class would not normally set foot in. The result of these experiences was *The Condition of the Working Classes of England*, an amazing piece of writing that included shocking accounts of the lives of the poor. It had really impressed Marx and he was very pleased to meet with Engels again when he visited Paris in August 1844. They spent much of that time together, soon became firm friends and began collaborating on pieces of writing.

Their first writing together was supposed to be a short critique of Bruno Bauer and his followers but it ended up as a 200-page booklet, most of it written by Marx. *The Holy Family* contained philosophy and literary criticism and defended the rights of workers, but really it was a bit of a rant by Marx attacking Bauer and his companions in the 'Free', as the Young Hegelians had become known.

Marx was now a notorious figure in France as well as Germany and the French authorities became uneasy. It only took a little persuasion from the Prussian government for them to expel Marx from France in 1845. He moved to Brussels, where Engels soon followed him having given up his job. They worked together on *The German Ideology*, which was the first time the materialist theory of history was defined in a structured way. It was not published until after Marx's death but he realized at the time that its main purpose had been to help him clarify his ideas.

Marx and Engels became involved in the League of the Just, a revolutionary secret society with a large German membership. These expatriates were led by Wilhelm Weitling, a German tailor who agreed with Auguste Blanqui, the French extremist who believed in revolution. He thought that the majority of workers would not be won over to communism and a minority would have to seize power on their behalf. The League was banned in France and so the headquarters were based in London, where eventually a large split grew between those who believed the ideas of Weitling and those who believed that the workers could be won over gradually through education and that communism would evolve peacefully.

By 1847 Marx and Engels were in control of the League and had turned it from a secret society into an open organization called The Communist League. At the second meeting of the League in December, Marx and Engels were asked to draw up the statutes of the League and write a statement of principles, or **manifesto**. The League already had a slogan, 'Working men of all countries, unite!'

The Communist Manifesto

The aim of the Communist League was to overthrow the old bourgeois society and Marx and Engels had to write some kind of document that would make their objectives clear. Unfortunately, Marx did not concentrate on the task straight away and it was only when he received a letter from the committee threatening 'that measures would be taken against him' if he didn't deliver the goods that he got on with it. It was finally finished in February 1848 and opens with the words, 'A spectre is haunting Europe – the spectre of communism'.

It is one of the earliest socialist writings and despite seeming dated and rather quaintly archaic in style it is still in print today and has some contemporary relevance. Although Marx had discussed the *Manifesto* with Engels and Engels had made several attempts at writing a version of it, the final document is almost entirely the work of Marx himself and it is here that Marxism can be seen in its embryonic form.

The Communist Manifesto:

- ▶ *describes the capitalist system that existed at that time and explains how it came about*
- ▶ *describes the* **proletariat** *and how it was created*
- ▶ *examines the conflict between the proletariat and the* **bourgeoisie**
- ▶ *puts forward the idea of* **revolution**
- ▶ *explains how communism might work in practice.*

It ends with the words, 'The proletarians have nothing to lose but their chains. They have a world to win. Working men of all countries unite!' and it is one of the most famous of all revolutionary texts. It was written as an appeal to the workers and so it has the feel of propaganda. The ideas in it are discussed in much more detail throughout this book.

Exile

Marx had already been exiled from Germany and from France and now that *The Communist Manifesto* had been published the Belgian authorities began to look on him with suspicion. The year 1848 was exciting for Marx and Engels, for not long after the *Manifesto* was published revolutions and uprisings began in many European cities. King Louis Philippe abdicated in February 1848 as a result of the new unrest sweeping through France. A new French Republic was proclaimed. Could this be the start of the revolutions that Marx and Engels had hoped for?

Prussian police spies had been watching Marx; in April 1847 the Prussian ambassador in Brussels had demanded the suppression of the journal he was editing and now that uprisings had begun the authorities wanted him out of the country.

In March 1848, a decree signed by King Leopold I of Belgium ordered him out of the country never to return. Marx was not particularly upset by this as he had already considered returning to life in France. The official who had signed the form ordering his expulsion from Paris had been dismissed and Marx had been invited back by an old socialist comrade Ferdinand Flocon, who was now a member of the provisional government.

Despite his willingness to leave, he was arrested on trumped-up charges of not having a proper passport and thrown into a prison cell. Although this was the official reason for his imprisonment, it is likely that it had more to do with his funding of dissident Germans working in Belgium. Some of the money ended up being used to buy guns, knives and other weapons – no wonder the authorities were nervous. Jenny Marx was also imprisoned under very wide-reaching vagrancy laws and although both of them were acquitted by a jury the next day, they were given only a few hours to leave the country. They had to quickly sell all their possessions before being taken to the French border under police escort.

Marx arrived in Paris on 5 March and he and Engels, inspired by the French example, soon began working towards a German revolution. They amended *The Communist Manifesto* into *The Demands of the Communist Party in Germany* and distributed it as far as they could.

Marx realized that he needed to be back in Germany in order to be more effective and so he decided to move back to Cologne. He still had contacts there and he hoped some of them would help in his new endeavour, a paper to be called *Neue Rheinische Zeitung*. When he arrived in Cologne he reported to the authorities and asked them to renew his Prussian citizenship but they refused. Engels returned to his family hoping that he could persuade them to finance this new venture but they did not.

Scraping together money, including Marx's family inheritance, they managed to publish the first issue in June 1848 and the paper soon had a large circulation. Some of this was due to the style of the paper, which was daring and often witty. In contrast to the other more dry and rambling philosophical German papers it was informative and came to the point. This did not go down well with the authorities as revolutionary uprisings were beginning throughout Germany and there were street fights in Berlin. A campaign of police harassment against the paper and its editors began. In October 1848 Engels left for Belgium where he was arrested and deported to France and the paper suspended publication for a few weeks.

When Engels returned, he and Marx were put on trial for 'insulting the public prosecutor'. No sooner did they get off this charge through Marx's brilliant and witty defence, than Marx was re-arrested on charges of 'incitement to revolt' for encouraging people to resist paying taxes, using force if necessary. Again, he was acquitted. Because he had been acquitted twice Marx began to feel that he was above the law and he still continued to write articles that upset the authorities and became even more daring. This was too much and the authorities pounced on the paper in May 1848, closed it down and prosecuted the workforce. All non-Prussians were to be deported and as Marx had not been able to get his citizenship renewed this included him. Everything was sold up, the family silver went into pawn and Marx and his family moved to Paris.

Paris was now totally changed from the city that he had left only recently. There had been a royalist reaction to the revolution and all foreign revolutionaries were to be evicted. Marx had hardly arrived when armed police came to the door to banish him to a rural part of Brittany; as Jenny was pregnant she was allowed another month to follow him. Marx did not wish to live in what he considered to be a swamp in the middle of nowhere. He could not go back to Germany or Belgium, he tried going to Switzerland but they wouldn't give him a passport, so he got on the next ship to Dover in England.

THINGS TO REMEMBER

▶ *Karl Marx was born on 5 May 1818 at Trier in Germany, which was then part of Prussia.*

▶ *The Industrial and French Revolutions meant that Europe was going through major social and political upheavals at that time.*

▶ *Not much is known about Marx's early childhood.*

▶ *He was intelligent and witty in character but sometimes moody and irritable and often fell out with friends.*

▶ *He studied law at university but changed to the study of philosophy.*

▶ *On leaving university he began work as a journalist and soon came to the notice of the authorities with his controversial writings on the plight of peasants.*

▶ *He married Jenny von Westphalen, the daughter of a cultured and aristocratic family friend, in 1843.*

▶ *In 1843 he moved to Paris where he mixed with radicals and revolutionaries and joined the Communist League.*

▶ *Friedrich Engels became his life long friend and co-writer at this time and together they wrote* The Communist Manifesto *in 1847.*

▶ *Marx was exiled from France, Prussia and Belgium and so he moved to England.*

2

Marx's later life

In this chapter you will learn:
* *key facts about Marx's later life and work in London*
* *about his friendship and working partnership with Engels*
* *about his work on* **Das Kapital** *and with the International*
* *about the end of his life.*

The move to London

When Marx moved to London in 1849 he only expected to be there for a few months at the most. As things turned out he ended up living there until his death in 1883 nearly 35 years later. He was buried in Highgate cemetery, so it could be claimed that he never left London.

London welcomed many refugees and was a place of sanctuary for many political dissidents. It was the largest city in the world at that time and there was a marked contrast between the lives of the rich and the poor.

The world of the poor was a sprawling industrial wilderness filled with factories spewing out smoke, sewers that poured into the river Thames and slum housing where people crowded together in unhygienic conditions without clean drinking water or proper toilets. Disease was rife, cholera epidemics were frequent and mortality rates were high.

Marx observed this world at first hand. His early years in London were spent in poverty and this had some effect on his family life. Three of his children died and one was stillborn. Although this was not uncommon at the time in all social classes, it was most often the poor who died young. Marx's own life and his observation of the lives of those around him meant that his writing about poverty was often vivid and full of hatred against a system that allowed people to live in such terrible conditions.

It must have been particularly hard for Jenny, his wife, to come to terms with the reduction in their circumstances as she was used to an aristocratic life of wealth and privilege. In September 1849 she arrived in London with their three young children, Jenny (Jennnychen), Laura and Edgar and was heavily pregnant with their fourth child. He was born on Guy Fawkes Night, 5 November. Marx rather liked the idea that his son was born on the day commemorating an attempt by revolutionaries to blow up the Houses of Parliament and named him Heinrich Guido in memory of the chief conspirator. He was often known in family circles as Fawkesy.

Family life in London

Marx is such a well-known icon that it is easy to forget he was also a human being and a family man. At first, the family lived in various temporary lodgings around Soho, where many other refugees lived. They were evicted on one occasion and the bailiffs came round and took all their meagre possessions, including the children's toys. They left Jenny Marx nursing little Fawkesy on bare boards, while their furniture was put onto the pavement outside.

Poor Fawkesy was a sickly child and prone to convulsions and he died in December 1850. By this time Jenny Marx was pregnant again and their daughter Franziska was born in March 1851.

Franziska died when she was just a year old after a bout of severe bronchitis and her father could not afford to pay for the funeral. A kindly French neighbour finally lent the family money to hire an undertaker and see that she was laid to rest with dignity.

The family moved to more permanent lodgings at 28 Dean Street at the end of 1850. These were at the top of the house and were only two rooms. They must have been very cramped for a man and wife, children, a housekeeper (Helene Demuth) and sometimes a male secretary (Wilhelm Pieper). Helene Demuth, known as Lenchen, became pregnant and it is alleged that Karl Marx was the father of her son.

The boy, born in June 1851, was known as Freddy Lewis Demuth. He was given to foster parents and lived most of his life in Hackney, London. There was no father's name on his birth certificate and many people at the time believed that Engels was the father, although the boy was said to look very like Marx. Engels said in later life that he had only let this story be circulated because he wanted to spare the Marx family from embarrassment. Although there is no conclusive proof, there are several family letters that hint at the paternity of the boy and most academics now believe that Freddy was indeed the son of Marx. It is no wonder that a Prussian police spy reported that Marx was living the life of a 'real bohemian'.

The Marx family had been systematically spied on by agents of the Prussian police because they were believed to be dangerous revolutionaries who wanted to bring down the governments of several European states and guillotine their ruling classes and monarchs. As Jenny's half-brother Ferdinand von Westphalen was the Prussian interior minister there was also an element of bad family feeling involved. He had been against her marriage to Marx in the first place.

These spies were not very efficient and Marx and Engels usually managed to spot them as they followed them or loitered about taking notes. They were not fooled by attempts to invite them into fake conspiracies either. However, one spy did infiltrate their household and wrote a report about the terribly dirty state of the place and of Marx in particular, who he describes as being an unwashed, heavy-smoking, heavy-drinking individual who kept irregular hours. Visitors wrote that the place was in a state of chaos with broken furniture, papers scattered everywhere, books, pipes, tobacco and toys lying about, all covered in a layer of dirt.

The bohemian air of the house was added to by the many visitors and members of the Communist League who dropped in for political discussion with Marx day and night. It was further cramped because Marx employed a secretary to help keep his papers in order, even though he had little money to pay him and the young man, Wilhelm Pieper, was not very efficient.

Pieper fancied himself as a rather flamboyant Byronesque Romantic and although he was supposed to translate papers for Marx, his translations were so bad that Engels usually redid them. Jenny Marx did not think much of him and was convinced that she could do his work easily and save the family some money, but Marx rather liked the idea of a secretary, even if he was useless and disappeared on romantic adventures time and time again. Pieper lived with the Marx family on and off for several years and often shared a bed with Marx because conditions were so overcrowded. Finally he left to become a teacher and Jenny was able to prove that she was an excellent secretary at last.

It was in this strange household that the children grew up, often living on a diet of nothing but bread and potatoes for days on end. Marx was not able to pay the bills on many occasions and could not afford to buy medicine when the family were ill. There was no kind of welfare state at that time and doctors' bills and medicines had to be paid for. The poor conditions and lack of good food meant that the family fell ill frequently. There were no antibiotics then either so infections took hold of people very quickly and they died of illnesses which are easily cured today.

All through his life Marx was dogged with a bad chest and had recurrent bouts of bronchitis. He was a heavy smoker and often joked that the money he made from *Das Kapital* was not enough to pay for the cigars he smoked while producing it. He suffered from carbuncles which he complained about frequently in his correspondence; these were boils that flared up when he was angry or stressed and sometimes they were so bad that he could not sit down. They were probably made worse by poor diet and his liver problems caused by drinking too much. He also suffered from what would probably be called stress today. Trying to support a family, write, and organize a political movement led to bouts of insomnia and headaches, which recurred repeatedly.

Marx became a frequent visitor to the pawn shop where he took the family silver his wife had inherited, and sometimes even the coat off his back, to raise a little cash. On one occasion he was imprisoned overnight because it was believed that the scruffy little refugee who came to pawn such fine silver must have stolen it. He was only released when Jenny went to the police to explain. Engels was a great help to them at this time and he sent money from the offices of his father's factory to try and keep them solvent.

When creditors and angry tradesmen came to the door Marx would often send his children down to tell them he was not in. Little Edgar was especially good at throwing them off the scent and, as the only boy, he was his father's favourite. Family life was chaotic but warm-hearted as Marx delighted in his children and spent a lot of time with them, which was unusual in those times. They all called him by his old nickname of Moor. He read the classics and Shakespeare to them and made up fairy tales and stories about the poor triumphing over evil landlords.

Another child was born in 1855, a daughter named Eleanor, who was a frail and ill child. At the time of her birth Edgar was only six years old and he also became very ill and weak with some kind of fever. Doctors eventually confirmed that he had consumption, as tuberculosis was called then. This is a highly infectious disease and at that time there was no cure. Edgar wasted away and died in April 1855.

Although the whole family was grief-stricken, Marx took Edgar's death very badly and could not be consoled. Engels took the family on a short holiday, but on their return the sight of Edgar's toys lying around made Jenny and Marx even more upset and they decided they had to move away from the place that had seen the deaths of three of their children. A blue plaque now commemorates their life there.

They moved to a much bigger house in a nicer part of London, near Hampstead Heath. This was only possible because one of Jenny's uncles had died and left them some money and shortly afterwards her mother died. It meant that they could redeem their possessions from the pawn shop and live a life of more ease. The girls all went to a private school and had dancing lessons as befitted young ladies of the time. These were happier times for the children as they had a garden where Marx often played with them, carrying them on his back like a horse. Sometimes they would go to the heath for picnics and laugh at their father when he hired a donkey and rode around the park on it.

Jenny Marx gave birth to a stillborn child not long after they moved in and she found that the house was isolated compared to the bustle in the centre of the city. She felt very run down for a long time and quite lonely, especially as the older girls were now at school and Marx was busy with his writing and socialist meetings.

The family still drifted in and out of debt and sometimes the girls couldn't go to school because their clothes were at the pawn shop. Engels kept them going with as much money as he could send. He was always a true friend to the family even though Jenny Marx did not really approve of him.

Marx and Engels

When Marx was expelled from Prussia in the summer of 1849 he began to rely more and more on his friendship with Engels. Engels was an excellent linguist; he claimed he could stammer in 12 languages, and Marx relied on him a great deal to help with translations. It was a friendship that lasted for 40 years, quite a surprising length of time considering Marx's volatile personality. He often fell out with people he had declared to be his close companions and Engels remained his one and only true friend. It helped that Engels had a fairly easy-going nature and idealized Marx and his intelligence. In later years he wrote to a friend, 'I simply cannot understand how anyone can be envious of genius'.

Engels, for all his intelligence, could not write with the same imaginative flair as Marx and he was happy to help him in any way he could in order to further the cause which they both believed in. He was a well-organized and clear writer though, and his *The Condition of the Working Classes in England* had greatly impressed Marx and influenced some of his writing. Their working partnership was a useful one because Engels enabled Marx to put some of his more fanciful and chaotic thoughts into simpler and more orderly fashion.

Engels was a generous benefactor to the Marx family and to the many other people in his life; he gave money for the upkeep of

Marx's illegitimate son for example. He lived in a ménage à trois with his mistress Mary Burns, a beautiful Irish redhead, and her sister Lizzie. He was also very generous to their family. He never seemed to complain about supporting all these people even when he had to embezzle money from the office cash box in order to keep up his financial commitments.

The only bad feeling between Marx and Engels came when Mary died. Marx appeared unsympathetic and asked for money in his letter of condolence, because he was about to be declared bankrupt. It was insensitive to say the least, but Marx soon apologized and the two became friends once again.

Engel's money came from his father, a rich textile merchant who had a branch of his business, Ermen and Engels, in Manchester at the heart of the industrial North of England. He first worked there in 1842 and it was then that he met Mary, who was a Chartist and a strong supporter of the rights of factory workers.

Insight

Chartism was one of the first mass working-class **labour** movements in the United Kingdom. It grew in popularity after the publication of the *People's Charter* in 1838. This asked for changes to the voting system including giving the vote to all men over 21.

It was his involvement with Mary that led to some of his writing about the conditions of the working classes. Engels reluctantly went back to work in Manchester in 1850 with the aim of helping Marx financially. He stayed there for 20 years until the closure of the factory meant that he could return to live in London permanently.

He managed to keep most of his socialist activities and his 'secret' household hidden from his parents; he appeared to be nothing much more than a local businessman to many people who knew him. His father gave him an entertainment and hospitality allowance, a lot of which ended up in the Marx household.

However he did ride with the Cheshire hunt and entertained guests at his respectable house, one where his mistress was never seen. Jenny Marx could not approve of his way of life, she always referred to Mary as 'your wife'; she did not refer to Lizzie at all.

The Marx family always called Engels 'General', a nickname he acquired due to his interest in military strategy and time spent in the armed forces. Letters passed between them all very frequently and give an interesting insight into their private lives. Marx and Engels kept no secrets from each other and even invented their own code language in order to keep their correspondence free from the prying eyes of police spies. Most of the letters have personal as well as political details in them as Engels also liked to gossip and write about his favourite hobbies: wine, beer, women and song!

In addition to working at the family business, Engels helped Marx write articles for the *New York Tribune,* a radical newspaper that had a large circulation in the USA. Marx did not write very good English when he arrived in London and Engels, as usual, came to his rescue. He helped out with translation and even wrote some of the articles, especially those that needed his expertise in military affairs.

Engels wrote most of the entries that Marx should have written for the *New American Cyclopaedia*, which were commissioned by the editor of the *New York Tribune*. This became difficult when Engels fell ill and Marx had to pretend that his work had been lost in the post on its way to New York.

Engels was one of the few people who could read Marx's handwriting and so it was naturally he, with the help of Eleanor Marx, who came to sort out Marx's papers after he died. Engels found that he was now the authority on communism and he went on to complete the further volumes of *Das Kapital* that Marx had intended to write. He became the interpreter for all that Marx had said or written and kept up an enormous correspondence until his death in 1895.

Work in London

Marx never had a 'proper' job while he lived in London, even though the family were sometimes destitute. On the one occasion he applied for a job, as a railway clerk, he was rejected because of his handwriting, which was completely illegible. He dedicated most of his time to the cause of communism and to writing the book that later became *Das Kapital* and Engels was quite happy to support him financially whenever he was able.

Marx did have some regular income as he was paid £1 per article (quite a good sum in those days) for his pieces in the *New York Tribune*, even though Engels helped out with a lot of the work. Marx became a popular journalist with the American readership of the *Tribune* and wrote for it on a weekly basis for ten years. His articles were witty and often vitriolic in nature against those who had offended him, for Marx kept his fiery temperament until late in his life and it often showed in his writing. He wrote about English politics and social analysis: articles on Chartism, foreign policy, the British rule in India and Ireland, economics, nationalism and land enclosures in Scotland, for example.

He also wrote for the *Neue Rheinische Zeitung (Revue)* a political economy review sold in Germany and London. It was managed and financed by Conrad Schramm, another German who was sympathetic to the revolutionary cause. The *Revue* did not sell well as it had only a small circulation among German revolutionaries and exiles and it only ran for five issues. Marx hardly made any money from this but he did make some money from the *New American Cyclopaedia* entries, even though Engels did much of the work.

Marx was always busy, even if his work was unpaid. One of his unpaid roles involved helping out with the German Workers Education Society. He was an inspiring teacher, although a little intimidating to some of his young students. He gave lectures which were often packed out with people impressed by his oratory and political invective. One series of lectures, which was filled to capacity, was on the subject 'What is bourgeois property?' He attended weekly discussion groups and also lectures on subjects ranging from astronomy to languages. Singing and dancing and musical entertainment were also available for the German refugees who made up most of the membership of the German Workers Education Society. Marx was fond of fencing and joined a club of French émigrés where he could practise his swordsmanship. He obviously hadn't been put off by the duel earlier in his life during which he was wounded.

Within a few days of arriving in London he met with other refugees and began to set up London headquarters for the Communist League. He was soon to be one of its most dominant members due to the force of his charismatic and intense personality; this was one of the reasons that a split formed in the League and it was eventually dissolved. Marx did not like having to work on projects where he was not in control, and when his ideas clashed with those of others he was likely to fly into rages and denounce them. He spent a great deal of time that he could have spent working on *Das Kapital*, writing lengthy diatribes against those who he believed had wronged him in some way. An example of this was his campaign against Karl Vogt. Vogt had written a book denouncing Marx as a lover of the aristocracy who wanted nothing but personal power. The book was not printed in London but Marx went into a white hot rage and, as he couldn't afford to sue for libel, he wrote a book in return, denouncing Vogt and anyone who had ever supported him.

These numerous distractions led him away from what he believed to be his true purpose, the writing of *Das Kapital*.

Das Kapital

Nearly every day of his life in London Marx would turn up at the reading room of the British Library to work on his writing. He often stayed there for 12 hours and wrote again at home into the small hours of the morning. This was the writing which eventually became *Das Kapital* or *Capital* as it is sometimes known in England. Volume one was finally finished in August 1867, but even then Marx continued revising and refining his work, making notes for the sequel he intended to publish. His letters are full of references to the toll that this work took on him. He was forever predicting that he was about to complete it but then finding he had more to write about.

Marx considered *Das Kapital* to be a scientific study of capitalism, politics and economics. He used the government Blue Books that were available at the Library to gather first-hand evidence on the plight of the poor. These contained statistics, census figures and reports from factory and public health inspectors. Engels had used these as a source for *The Condition of the Working Classes in England*. Marx was impressed by this and decided to use them in a similar way in his masterwork.

Opinion is divided over the merits of *Das Kapital*. Many people find it a very difficult read. Marx was fond of satirical puns and he uses many literary references which are not easily understood by the general reader of today.

Insight

Insight into the literary background of *Das Kaptial* can be found in Francis Wheen's book *Marx's Das Kapital: A Biography*.

Das Kapital is very long with a lot of footnotes, which can be off-putting to anyone first opening the book. The footnotes are some of the most interesting bits, in my opinion, because it is there that Marx gives some of the first-hand accounts of the lives of working people and they give a fascinating glimpse into our industrial past. One example, taken from a Children's Employment Commission Report of 1865, is of children walking the equivalent of 15–20 miles every six hours in a bottle factory while continually performing their work. They were not allowed meal breaks as the furnace would cool down and their shifts were often 14 or 15 hours long.

Engels tried to get Marx to change the format of *Das Kapital* because he could see that it opened with difficult abstract concepts. 'It is dreadfully tiring and confusing too', he wrote, when shown the proofs. He thought Marx should have broken up the chapters into much shorter sections with headings to make the book easier to read. Marx did not take much notice of his comments.

The publication of *Das Kapital* brought Marx a great deal of personal satisfaction but it did not have the huge reception that he had hoped for. Engels, ever the true friend, sent false reviews to German papers with the hope that they might stir up some public opinion but to no avail. There were a few favourable reviews in the British press but the book did not have mass sales or lead to any type of political action by workers as Marx had hoped.

The first nine chapters of the book deal with the explanation of Marx's economic theory in rather abstract terms, while the rest of the book explores the evidence that shows the ways in which capitalists exploit their workers. Marx uses a lot of historical examples for he believed that capitalism was a stage in a process of social history that was inevitably and ultimately leading to its own downfall. For those who find *Das Kapital* a difficult read, the basics of Marx's economic theory can be found in the works *Value, Price and Profit* and *Wage-labour and Capital*. These were based on lectures given to working men's associations and are much easier to understand. The ideas in *Das Kapital* are discussed in more detail in Chapter 5.

The International

One of the other distractions that took Marx away from his writing was his involvement with The International Workingmen's Association. The International, as it became known, was founded in 1864 at a public meeting to which Marx was invited. Until then, workers throughout Europe and America had been concentrating on their own struggles, without much thought for others in similar situations worldwide. It was French and British trade unionists who finally realized that there would be strength in numbers and that they would all reach their aims more efficiently if they banded together.

The first meeting took place in London at St Martin's Hall and the chairman was Edward Beesly, a professor of ancient history, who was also a radical and a supporter of trade unions. The meeting voted in favour of forming a constitution for an international federation that would work towards destroying the current system of economic relations. They intended to replace this with a system where workers owned the **means of production,** leading to the end of exploitation, a sharing out of the profits and the end of private property.

Marx was voted onto the executive committee as the representative of the German artisans and by the time of the second meeting, when the constitution was drawn up, he had effectively taken control. Marx did not usually like to be associated with groups that he had not initiated himself. It was well known that he preferred to be in control of everything and he only made the exception of going to the first meeting because he had great respect for Edward Beesly. He also believed strongly in the principles of the workers and could see that they had been greatly influenced by his own writing.

He managed to obtain a great degree of control because the delegates who had been issued with the task of writing the constitution failed to do a good job and he took over and wrote the constitution and inaugural address himself. The address began with the words 'The emancipation of the working class must be conquered by the working class themselves'.

The constitution was a daring statement at the time, for the International members were pledged to assist one another in improving their 'common condition' and to subvert and possibly overthrow the existing capitalist regime by open political action. They were to do this by democratic means where possible by trying to enter parliament. The foundations of the British Labour Party and many European socialist parties can be traced back to the work of the early International, although Marx did not see these formed in his lifetime.

Marx also included a short survey of economic and social conditions in his inaugural address, showing that the ruling classes benefited by setting workers against the workers in other countries. He pointed out that wars only benefited the ruling class and not the ordinary man. He concluded that in order to make changes in the system the workers should protest, demonstrate and harass their governments. It was up to the workers to make changes in the existing social structure for they were the only class that this would benefit. The address finished with the words famous from *The Communist Manifesto*, 'Workers of the world unite'.

The aims of the International were to establish close relations and co-operation between workers in various countries and close relations between different trades and trade unions, which up until then had often worked against each other. This was to be achieved by collecting relevant statistics and passing information on the conditions, needs and plans of workers from one country to another. There were also to be discussion groups, publication of regular reports and international co-ordination in times of crisis. Yearly meetings were to be convened by a democratically elected council.

Marx found that he became a well-known public figure, among socialist circles at least, and much of his time was soon taken up by the International. It grew rapidly as more and more unions joined and it was efficient and well organized. He dominated the meetings and writings of the International because of his vast experience and his forceful personality. There was no one else in the group who could really match his intelligence and idealism and his work for them took up his nights and days, although he was not paid. He did not usually attend the meetings of the congress for he preferred to stay in London at the centre of operations, dealing with correspondence and issuing orders.

This finally led to a dispute with Bakunin, the Russian anarchist leader. Marx and Bakunin were old enemies. Marx had a habit of enthusiastically embracing people only to utterly reject them later when they disagreed with his theories. Both men grudgingly admired the intellect of the other but there was a great personal animosity between them. As can be seen later, in Chapter 3, Bakunin believed that the only way for the workers to be freed from the chains of capitalism was by violent means and the destruction of all governments.

Bakunin wanted the International to be run more loosely as a federation of semi-independent local bodies and he had followers in Italy and Switzerland. They decided to form a splinter group, loosely affiliated to the International but with its own organizational structure. This went against the principles of the International, which was supposed to be a united party. Marx finally had Bakunin and his supporters expelled from the International after they became affiliated with a Russian terrorist, Nechaev.

Marx fell out of favour with many members of the International during the time of the Franco-Prussian War and the Paris Commune of 1870. The Paris Commune was a result of a revolution that occurred when the National Guard, a volunteer citizens' force, took over Paris. They deposed government officials and elected a revolutionary committee which they said was the true government of France.

Insight

Paris came under siege in 1870 as a result of war with Prussia. This caused terrible hardship and led to the formation of a short-lived government of the people known as the Paris Commune. It existed formally between March and May 1871 before being overthrown. In this short time the Communards, as they were called, had begun implementing social policies of separating the church and state and giving the right to employees to take over business enterprises. They also planned to make education and training free for all citizens.

It was not a communist revolution but it was one of the first examples of open class war ever to take place. Workers, soldiers, artists, writers, all manner of free thinkers, joined forces to overthrow a rule that they saw as unjust. There was mass hysteria and the Communards had only vague plans of how they would rule after the initial violent revolution had taken place. Paris was besieged by troops and a reign of terror began. Food ran out, innocent people were blamed and hostages were guillotined, including the archbishop of Paris. Many of the middle classes believed the Communards to be a bunch of criminally insane thugs and their actions horrified the bourgeois citizens of Europe, even those in the International who welcomed revolution.

Marx, however, wrote a pamphlet, *The Civil War in France*, in which he applauded the measures the Communards had taken and said they had not gone far enough. It brought notoriety to the members of the International and they were publicly identified with violence and outrageous behaviour. This was not in keeping with the beliefs expressed in their constitution and many members blamed Marx for bringing the group into disrepute. This led to factions being set up in the group and weakened its power.

The International finally fizzled out in 1876 after the council was transferred to the USA at Marx's request. He felt there was still a lot of bad feeling towards him since his writing on the Commune and this was a way of winding everything down without explicitly having to do so. He knew he could not keep control over its affairs and warring factions for ever and if he couldn't be in control he didn't want to be involved. He admitted privately to friends that he felt tired and it was all wearing him out. Although the members were shocked and stunned they voted to have the headquarters move to the USA by a small majority. The US socialist movement was remote from the European one and without their support it fell into disrepute. The International was reconvened later after Marx's death but by then it was much more conciliatory in nature than it had been when Marx was alive.

The later years

Marx became much less of a public figure after the International was dissolved. He spent a lot of time writing and he saw Engels frequently after his move to London. They were now the world authorities on **socialism**.

Insight

At the time Marx and Engels were writing, the terms socialism and communism were almost interchangeable, meaning a society where there was collective ownership of goods and equality for all. For Marx, socialism was the stage before true communism.

As Marx grew older he lost some of his fiery temper and did not write the vitriolic attacks on his opponents that he had in the past. Visitors who came to see him were surprised that he seemed such a genial man, for his reputation had portrayed him as a morose and irritable monster.

Marx took great pleasure from his grandchildren and spent a lot of time with them. Jennychen had married Charles Longuet, a French socialist who lectured at London University, and they had five sons. Laura married another Frenchman, Paul Lafargue, also a socialist. They had three children who all died.

Eleanor did not marry and stayed at home. She wanted to be an actress, which was not a very reputable profession in those days and she scandalized people by smoking, something a respectable young woman did not do. She was the daughter who was most like Marx in temperament and looks, with very dark, piercing eyes. She also shared his nervous health problems and together they visited spas around Europe looking for a cure for their skin and lung problems. These were probably not helped by the fact that they both chain-smoked, even when taking treatments.

Jenny Marx became seriously ill in 1880 and the family went to Ramsgate for a seaside rest, something that was very popular at that time. Her health did not improve and she became terribly emaciated. It was found she had cancer and she lived with a great deal of pain until her death in December 1881. Marx could not even go to her funeral for he was terribly ill with bronchitis at the time.

Engels said that Marx was now 'effectively dead'. He did not have the strength to write much and relied on Eleanor as his companion but she was suffering from a kind of nervous exhaustion brought on by her thwarted ambition. She was desperate to go on stage but remained with her father. He had not approved of the man she wished to marry and she lived under a kind of mental pressure that drove her into times when she starved herself and lived off nothing but tea. Marx realized that he had to let her live her own life and after that he spent time visiting Europe and North Africa, trying to find a climate that would improve his health. His lungs were in a very poor state and he was diagnosed with chronic bronchitis.

By 1883 he was very weak and tired and when his favourite daughter, Jennychen, died of bladder cancer he seemed to finally lose the will to live. He had not seen the revolutionary changes that he had hoped for and did not know that they would ever occur. He felt despair that most of his work had been for nothing. When Eleanor went to France to help with the Longuet children she said she believed her father had gone home to die. He had bronchitis and pleurisy with abscesses on his lungs and was too weak even to read. Engels was terribly worried about him and visited often.

On 14 March 1883 Engels visited and was told by Lenchen that Marx was dozing by the bedroom fire in his favourite armchair. By the time Engels went upstairs Marx was dead.

He was buried in Highgate cemetery. Only 11 mourners were at the grave, and a short paragraph in *The Times* obituary column noted his passing. He was not well known or respected, except in socialist circles, and few people believed that anything he had said would have any effect on the world around them.

THINGS TO REMEMBER

▶ *Marx moved to London after his exile in 1849, intending to stay for only a few months, but lived there until his death.*

▶ *Marx and his family lived in poverty for a lot of that time and of his seven legitimate children only three survived into adulthood.*

▶ *Marx relied greatly on the support of Engels both financially and with his writing.*

▶ *Marx spent most of his days at the British Library working on* Das Kapital *as well as working for the International.*

▶ Das Kapital *was his attempt to make a scientific study of politics, economics and capitalism. It was not well received at the time.*

▶ *He died in 1883 in some obscurity and only 11 mourners attended his funeral.*

3

Marx and philosophy

In this chapter you will learn:
- *about the philosophers who came before Marx*
- *about political economists and Utopian Socialists*
- *how they influenced his thinking*
- *how he differed from them.*

Marx is seen by some as a great philosopher and by others as a great economist. He was in fact both of these things, although he claimed to have little time for most of the philosophers who went before him: 'The philosophers have only interpreted the world in different ways; the point is to change it', he wrote in a thesis on Feuerbach, the German philosopher. This is sometimes seen as a statement that he was totally against the study of philosophy and saw it as a waste of time. In fact, he believed that philosophy should be made clearer by scientific study and then used to bring about social change.

His interest in the serious study of philosophy began while at the university in Berlin. His doctoral thesis was written on the contrasts between two ancient Greek philosophers: Democritus and Epicurus. Marx saw parallels between the thoughts of these ancient philosophers and the interpretation of Hegel's philosophy. Hegel was an important figure in Germany at that time and his ideas were hotly debated by students, who have always enjoyed sitting around discussing what a terrible state the world is in and how they would like to change it. When Marx's father accused him of 'debauchery in a dressing gown' he probably had no idea that his son would be one of the few students who would go on to change the world in a significant way.

The main debate among philosophers of the time centred around the differences between the views of idealist and materialist philosophers. To explain this very simply, **idealist philosophers** assume there is a divine force of some kind which is responsible for the development of ideas and beliefs among mankind; on the other hand, **materialist philosophers** believe that all ideas and beliefs come out of life and its conditions and not from any divine being or supernatural force.

The debate between idealists and materialists had been recorded from the time of the ancient Greeks but it had been renewed by the popularity of Hegel in Germany at the time Marx was a student. It is easier to understand the importance of the debate, and of the development of Hegel's philosophy by Marx, if we look at the development of Western philosophy up to the nineteenth century (the incorporation of Eastern philosophy into European thinking did not really begin until after the death of Marx, becoming popularized in the works of psychologist Carl Jung, 1875–1961, and Friedrich Nietzsche, 1844–1900).

A brief history of philosophy

As philosophy tries to explain the truth behind life itself it must have been around for as long as mankind has existed. The earliest people had no means of recording what they believed so we can only surmise that they were superstitious and tried to explain natural phenomena as products of some divine force. Natural elements such as fire and water were worshipped as gods and from this organized religion developed.

In the Western world, the first philosophers (as we understand the term today) were ancient Greeks who started by criticizing religious beliefs. They used the scientific knowledge that was available to them at the time to explain the world around them and this sometimes brought them into conflict with organized religion and led to persecution.

The conflict between organized religion and free-thinkers went on for centuries. In Europe the dominance of the Christian church did not encourage the development of philosophical thought. Anyone who did not agree with orthodox Christian doctrines was likely to be branded as a heretic and tortured to death.

It was not until the fifteenth century that freer debate began, and it was not until the French and American Revolutions in the eighteenth century that the Church began to lose its dominance over the thoughts of the masses.

The materialist philosophers of the eighteenth and nineteenth centuries debated the existence of God and whether this could be proved by scientific means. Scientific development at that time was in the fields of mathematics and mechanical laws, for example Newton's Laws of Motion. This influenced the world view of the philosophers who saw society as fixed and unchanging, believing it followed immutable scientific rules. It meant that people believed they had a fixed place in society which could not be altered. It was not until Hegel developed the idea of the **dialectic** that people began to understand that nothing was constant and that they themselves had a part to play in influencing the course of history.

Which philosophers influenced Marx?

Marx did not arrive at his own philosophy without studying, and being influenced by, those who went before him. He wrote, 'no credit is due to me for discovering the existence of classes ... nor yet the struggle between them'. Philosophers in the distant past, such as Aristotle, had seen the influence of class. Marx analysed the ideas of these ancient philosophers and read voraciously on many subjects. He also met many of the idealists and revolutionaries in Europe who wanted to change society. As he read and digested what they had to say, certain groups of thinkers became more important to him and became part of his own political and economic philosophy. Among these groups there were individuals whose ideas can be seen to have definitely influenced the philosophy of Marx.

Ancient Greek philosophers

The study of ancient Greek philosophy was an important part of the education of young Europeans in Marx's time. It became even more popular in Germany under the influence of Hegel. There were three main ancient Greek influences on Marx's philosophy.

Democritus (c460–c370BC) was an Greek materialist philosopher who believed that the world could be explained by scientific laws, although science at the time was not advanced enough for him to be able to prove his theory. He believed that matter was made up of atomic particles, despite there being no means of him proving this. This view of the world meant that he saw that everything was in motion and in a process of change. The majority of other philosophers had the view that matter was fixed and unchanging. This fixed view of the universe continued in mainstream philosophy up until the time of Hegel and influenced the way that people thought about the structure of the world, including institutions such as the Church and State.

Epicurus (341–271BC) was a Greek philosopher who believed that if the world operates on mechanical principles then death and the gods are not to be feared. He thought this freedom from fear would allow people to live in peaceful communes devoted to pleasure. His ideas influenced both Marx and Nietzsche.

Aristotle (384–322BC) was a Greek philosopher, scientist and teacher. He was very well read on many diverse subjects and wrote a huge number of philosophical works. He tried to integrate all knowledge into a unified philosophical system. It was not until Hegel wrote *The Science of Logic* in the nineteenth century that anyone else tried to encompass everything into a system of philosophy. Aristotle saw the universe as fixed and unchanging and it was his view that was taken up by the official Church and dominated Western philosophy until after the Middle Ages. He was one of the first people to write that conflict in society often comes from economic conditions and inequality in the structure of society; something that Marx was to develop later.

European philosophy

There are many philosophers in a great chain connected to each other through time, each building upon those who have gone before. The connections between the thoughts of philosophers and how they have all influenced each other would be a huge book, so

I can only write about a few of the philosophers who appear to have directly influenced what Marx wrote and the way in which he wrote it.

René Descartes (1596–1650), a French philosopher and mathematician, was the father of modern philosophy. He believed that philosophy and knowledge could be unified and classified by mathematical means. This was part of the inspiration for the scientific method that Marx attempted to apply to his historical researches.

John Locke (1632–1704) was an English philosopher and physician. He believed that religion did not hold the absolute truth and that knowledge 'is founded on and ultimately derives from sense'. His belief in social equality – 'we are all equal, of the same species and condition … with equal right to enjoy the fruits of nature' – and his belief that if the rulers of society offend against natural law they must be deposed, were to be a powerful influence on the American and French Revolutions.

Thomas Hobbes (1588–1679), an English philosopher and tutor, was one of the first people to try and study society scientifically in his book *Leviathan*, published in 1651. He was trying to understand human nature and the laws that governed it and as he favoured the views of Galileo and Gassendi, scientists who believed that the universe was in motion and the earth was not the centre of that motion, he was called a demon by the Catholic Church. His view of society was an authoritarian one: he believed there should be an absolute ruler. He thought that people need a social structure, for life in a state of nature (i.e. before society existed) is 'solitary, poor, nasty, brutish and short'.

Utopian Socialists

The word 'utopian', pertaining to an imagined perfect place, came into the English language in 1515 after the publication of *Utopia,* a book written by Thomas More, the English lawyer, author and statesman. Utopia was the name of the ideal state More envisaged, where private property had been abolished and religious tolerance was practised. More did not think that Utopia might actually come to exist; for him it was a literary device that meant he had the freedom to discuss controversial and heretical ideas in an age of religious intolerance. The **Utopian Socialists,** on the other hand, really believed that their ideal societies could be built.

The Utopian Socialists lived and wrote at the beginning of the nineteenth century and observed the changes in society that were occurring around them. Many people at that time believed that industrialization and the factory system had led to changes in society for the worse. Following the ideas of Jean-Jacques Rousseau, the French philosopher, such people wanted to return to some golden age in the past where life had been better. The Utopians totally disagreed: 'the golden age of the human race lies not behind but ahead of us', wrote Saint-Simon, one of the more well-known Utopians.

There was no specific movement that called itself Utopian Socialism – Marx and Engels were the first to use the term – but as the Utopian Socialists all lived around the same time and there are similarities in some of their ways of thinking it is valuable to consider them as a coherent group.

The three major Utopian Socialists who had an influence on Marx and Engels were Robert Owen, Charles Fourier and Claude Henri de Saint-Simon. Each of them envisaged their ideal society in a different way, and they were not always clear about the way in which these societies would come into being, but they were all in agreement that the social structure of the time was unfair, riddled with inequality and needed to be changed. This was not an entirely philanthropic view; many of the proposals of Utopian Socialists were led by a very real fear of revolution following the lead of recent upheavals in France. They had seen that if the social structure was not changed by those in power it could be overthrown from below.

Robert Owen (1771–1858) was a Welsh social reformer who believed character was formed by social conditions and that the greatest happiness of the greatest number should be the aim of society. Although he was a successful cotton manufacturer, he hated the factory system as it led to what he believed was destructive competition. He envisaged a whole society of 'villages of co-operation'. In 1800, as an experiment, he built a model community with schools and good housing for his mill workers at New Lanark in Scotland.

> **Insight**
> New Lanark is now a world heritage site and well worth a visit.

His workers enjoyed shorter working hours, after-hours recreational facilities, insurance plans and relatively safe and healthy working conditions. He also did away with child labour, but despite all this he still managed to make a profit. This made him very popular with other industrialists and New Lanark had many visits from all kinds of businessmen from around the world. The workers were still suspicious of him, for after all he was still the factory owner and he ruled over their lives in a very dominant patriarchal manner.

Owen believed that, once people had seen the example he set, villages on his model would spread rapidly throughout the country, but he couldn't get any financial backing privately or from the government and the experiment failed. He tried again in the USA, setting up New Harmony and several other Owenite communities, but these did not last more than a few years and they faded away after his death.

New Lanark was not a truly communist society in any sense of the word, for it was owned and directed by Owen and his partners; the workers had no democratic representation and it was driven by private property and the profit motive. The Owenite communities contained some early aspects of communal living and central organization, such as an attempt to abolish money and replace it with an exchange of labour, that were to be become important to later communism.

Charles Fourier (1772–1837) was a French social theorist who believed society should be reorganized into self-sufficient units or communes with communal property and consumer co-operatives for the redistribution of wealth. He totally rejected industrialization, unlike Owen who tried to improve it. Fourier was a rather bizarre visionary who had some rather strange and incoherent ideas, but among all these were some genuine flashes of insight about the human condition and the nature of society.

Fourier does not appear to have had any formal academic training and claims to have been bored by philosophers. Although born into a family of cloth merchants, he hated commerce, which he found demeaning, and he believed manual labour was degrading. He said that the factory system was dehumanizing and unnatural and that if God had intended us to work in such a way we would have been made to enjoy industriousness like ants or bees appear to. It was his assertion that work should be made pleasurable and enjoyable so that it became physically and mentally satisfying. Society should try to eliminate all unpleasant jobs, learning to live without products and services that no one wanted to make or do. This impressed Engels at the time and he wrote glowingly about him to Marx.

Fourier also believed that emotional ties were important, that people needed love and friendship as well as material possessions and satisfactions. In this way he was one of the first people to talk about the **alienation** that was later developed by Hegel and Marx.

Fourier's ideal society consisted of communities called phalanstèries with exactly 1,620 people living in them. This was so that a harmonious mix of the 810 personality types he believed in would be able to live happily under the Law of Passional Attractions he had invented. His communities foreshadowed a more 'liberated society', including sexual freedom and polyamorous relationships, for he believed that people were sexually repressed by religious rules. He was also a feminist (he invented the word), believing that women in nineteenth-century society were no better than slaves. In his society, women would be emancipated and have the right to have four husbands at once.

Insight

Modern feminists would not agree that having four husbands is in any way advantageous to women!

Fourier did not give much indication of how this society might come about, but he was against revolution, having seen the effects of it at first hand in France.

Although some of his visions of the future utopia he called 'Harmony' are far fetched – for example there would be six moons orbiting the world and the seas would turn to lemonade – his psychological insights into the nature of work, society and alienation were an important innovation at the time that still has relevance today.

Claude Henri de Saint-Simon (1760–1825) was a French aristocrat who narrowly avoided the guillotine during the French Revolution. This made him a fervent believer in social progress without the need for revolution. He was a rather colourful figure who spent a lot of his time mixing with the higher social classes, intellectuals and artists. After a kind of breakdown he spent some time in an asylum for the insane. He was not a socialist but many of his followers became known as such. He believed that lessons about society could be learned from studying history in a systematic way and he was aware of the importance of class struggle throughout history. He saw that, although the aims of the French Revolutionaries had been 'liberty, fraternity and equality', society had become less equal as a result of the revolution, for the gap between rich and poor had widened. This was reflected in his view of society which he saw as being divided between the industriels (workers) and oisifs (the rich parasites who lived off them).

Saint-Simon believed that the upper class of kings, nobles and priests had served a function in the past that was no longer necessary because the Industrial Revolution had made it obsolete. He welcomed capitalism because it would bring forward great scientific progress which he believed was the key to the growth of society. Both Fourier and Owen saw capitalism and the Industrial Revolution as something evil that had changed society for the worse; their utopias were an attempt to make a type of rural, communal living popular. Saint-Simon, on the other hand, welcomed the technological changes that were happening and wished to exploit them. As he didn't have much experience of ordinary workers he believed that they were not capable of running society and his proposal for the future was to have an elite of technocrats in authority over them. The technocracy would consist of highly intelligent and creative people. After his death his followers divided up into several factions and some of them began to make his ideas more socialist in order to appeal to the workers: they advocated the abolition of the inheritance of private property for example.

Despite his elitism, Saint-Simon's ideas are an important step in the development of Marxism because he was the first person to fully appreciate how industrial change had transformed society and to see it as part of the whole historical perspective.

Revolutionaries and anarchists

Marx lived at a time of revolution; the French Revolution (1789–99) had not long ended when Marx was born and this was a pivotal period in the history of Europe. After the revolution, French society and religion went through radical changes and the whole society was restructured. Although France became a republic, then an empire, and finally returned to a monarchy in Marx's lifetime, it was obvious that the age of the aristocrats was over and the citizens, including workers, were now a political force to be reckoned with. Marx read many of the works of the revolutionaries and met with many of them during his exile in Paris. They did not always see eye to eye, for Marx was of the belief that revolution could not be forced upon people and it would happen when the time was right. This was a major problem with his relationship with the anarchists, for although they shared the same goal of a free classless society, the anarchists believed in direct action by the masses and a rejection of all forms of government.

Louis Auguste Blanqui (1805–81) was a French revolutionary and extremist who believed in violent revolution and was the first to speak of the power of the proletariat. He spent half his life in prison because of his revolutionary activities; he was not satisfied by the results of the French Revolution and went on trying to make changes in society despite opposition. He was the person who invented the phrase '**dictatorship of the proletariat**' which Marx later used in a slightly different way from Blanqui. Blanqui believed that future revolution would never occur unless professional revolutionaries took action on behalf of the workers. They would then take charge of the country and abolish religions as their first step towards a new society. Marx could not agree with Blanqui's elite of revolutionaries working in secret behind the scenes; he believed that the changes in society would come about as a result of the general will of the people and as a natural result of the decay of the capitalist system.

Pierre-Joseph Proudhon (1809–65) was a French philosopher and economist, and the first person to call himself an anarchist. He was a printer and journalist with some education, but his family did not have much money to pay for books and his early poverty led to a hatred of the landed rich. After he wrote *What is Property?* in 1840, Marx entered into correspondence with him and they became friends. Marx came to disapprove of Proudhon's anarchy and published vicious criticisms of him, writing *The Poverty of Philosophy* as a criticism of Proudhon's *The Philosophy of Poverty*. Their disagreement was one of the reasons for the split in the International.

Proudhon rejected both capitalism and communism and he invented a form of anarchism that he called mutualism.

This involved control of the means of production by the workers and a central bank that would give out interest-free loans. Workers would form co-operatives or be self-employed and would trade with each other freely. Factories were to be run by groups of workers under democratic principles. The state would be abolished and society would be organized by a federation of 'free communes'.

Proudhon is famous for the saying 'property is theft'. This cry was taken up by revolutionary communists and is often wrongly attributed to Marx.

Louis Blanc (1811–82) was a French socialist and a politician. He believed social equality should come about by democratic and peaceful means. He thought competition was one of the major evils in society and wanted to see a society where wages were equalized and workers were united into 'social workshops'. These were something like trade unions. He was exiled to Britain and, like Marx, he spent a lot of time in the British Museum reading and writing. His best known saying, 'From each according to his ability, to each according to his needs' was another cry taken up by revolutionary communists and often wrongly attributed to Marx.

Mikhail Bakunin (1814–76) was a Russian anarchist leader who eventually came into conflict with Marx. Like Marx he had become interested in philosophy as a student; he translated Hegel into Russian and travelled from his homeland to Berlin to study under him at the university. He met Marx in Paris in 1844 and also Proudhon, who became one of his close friends.

Bakunin was imprisoned in Russia for his part in trying to bring about an uprising of the Slavs and was eventually exiled to Siberia. From there he escaped to the USA via Japan and finally became very involved in the International. It was here that he came into conflict with Marx: they had a very personal hatred of each other, each one believing the other to be arrogant. Bakunin could agree with Marx on his analysis of the class system and with his economic theory but he totally disagreed with Marx's view of communism, believing it would only come about through revolution. He believed that communism was only the first step towards anarchism.

The importance of Hegel and Feuerbach

Marx was a German and so he was obviously influenced by the philosophers from his homeland, but at that time in history German philosophy was the root of a great tradition that spread worldwide. The repressive, authoritarian Prussian regime stamped out any kind of revolutionary activity but they couldn't stop the talk in cafés and bars. Philosophy flourished and the hottest name in philosophy at that time was that of Georg Wilhelm Friedrich Hegel. Marx was influenced by many different philosophers, thinkers and social reformers but the most important of them all was Hegel. His influence on Marx was profound. **Lenin** believed that it is impossible for anyone to understand *Das Kapital* if Hegel has not been read and understood first. Marx resisted Hegel's ideas when he first went to university but he soon converted to Hegel's philosophy, coming to reject most of it later when he developed his own ideas. However, even late in his life he said he was still indebted to the genius of Hegel.

GEORG WILHELM FRIEDRICH HEGEL

Georg Wilhelm Friedrich Hegel (1770–1831) was a German philosopher who believed civilization progressed through intellectual development and saw the history of society as a series of conflicts or 'dialectics'.

Hegel's philosophy is difficult to put into simple terms. It is often obscure and not related to the real world. Marx intended to make Hegel intelligible and rational to ordinary thinkers on a few sheets of paper, for he thought that Hegel's own words were too mystical and not rational enough, but sadly he never had time to do it. He and Engels were both impressed by the historical perspective of society that ran through Hegel's work.

Hegel studied to be a Lutheran Pastor at a theological college and it was here he met the visionary poet Friedrich Hölderlin who became his closest friend. Hölderlin was passionate about the ancient Greeks and introduced Hegel to their philosophy. When Hegel became a private tutor he had time to read and think and spend time observing the natural world and he began to write his own philosophy; his earliest work concerned free enterprise, economics and labour for he read the works of Adam Smith and other political economists. It is unlikely that Marx was able to read Hegel's earliest work but there is a strange synchronicity in the development of their thought at a young age: both of them were friendly with poets and loved literature but they concentrated their intellects on the works of political economists.

Hegel went on to teach philosophy to large classes and so he began to develop a scientific form or template for the understanding of philosophic thought. He was trying to construct a huge system of philosophy that was complete in itself and encompassed everything. *The Science of Logic* was finally published in three volumes beginning in 1812.

Hegel's philosophical arguments have two main strands. The first is that human civilization comes about through intellectual and moral progress and that this is due to some kind of rational spirit that exists in humanity (**universal mind**) and not through divine intervention. It is as if history was a book written by the universal mind and humans are just characters in a book that it has written. This appealed to people at the time: they could see history as something coherent, that everything has its place in the plot that has been written and that history has not been random or meaningless. Civilization was an intentional progress towards a fixed end, and that end was finalized in Prussian society in 1805.

The second strand is the development of the dialectic, that is, the idea that change comes about as a result of conflict between two opposing movements. Hegel realized that his dialectic philosophy (he called it speculative reason) was totally different from the

logical **syllogism** of Aristotelian philosophy; it differs from
Aristotle because it cannot be applied to everything or stated
in simple terms.

Insight

In a book of this length it is difficult to summarize thousands
of years of philosophical theory but anyone wishing a deeper
understanding could begin with *Understand Philosophy*.

Hegel believed that things only acquire their true meaning if we
see them as part of a process of change and that 'all things are
contradictory in themselves'.

He saw this development consisting of three stages of dynamic
movement, which are sometimes called **thesis, antithesis** and
synthesis, although he rarely used these terms himself. According to
Hegel, development happens in this way:

1 Thesis – *the original idea or form is set up. This is also known
  as the 'position'.*
2 Antithesis – *the second, contradictory viewpoint contradicts
  the first. This is also known as 'negation of the position'.*
3 Synthesis – *the amalgamation of the two opposing views
  occurs. A 'negation of the negation' occurs but does not
  cancel it out, for a whole is formed. The whole is formed by
  overcoming the thesis and antithesis but still preserves them as
  a part of its final form. Hegel called this Aufhebung which is
  sometimes translated as 'sublation'.*

In Hegel's view, ideas develop through contradiction. The original
idea, or thesis, is set up but is then contradicted and rejected by
the antithesis. Eventually, the best parts of both the thesis and
antithesis can be combined: this is called the synthesis. A synthesis
of ideas cannot take place until the first two stages have been
gone through. Because the synthesis is made from the amalgamation
of two opposing viewpoints it also must eventually be opposed
or rejected. A new idea will then take its place, to again
be contradicted.

WHEN SHALL WE THREE MEET AGAIN?

THESIS   ANTITHESIS   SYNTHESIS

Insight

It cannot be stressed enough that one of the most important parts of Marxist theory is the idea that the economy and society are inherently unstable because society is made of a synthesis of two opposing classes.

In Hegel's philosophy, ideas are constantly developing and changing and history progresses by learning from its mistakes. This contrasted with the beliefs of the materialist philosophers who went before: they believed that everything followed immutable natural laws, seeing man as a cog in a machine that he could not influence.

Marx later took this idea of the dialectic and applied it in a practical way to the development of society and the economy instead of to the purely philosophical world of ideas. He claimed that in Hegel's work the truth stood on its head and he had now put it the right way up by showing that ideas developed from the material world of economics; in other words, the conditions in which a person lives and works determine the way in which he thinks. This seems obvious to us today.

LUDWIG ANDREAS FEUERBACH

Ludwig Andreas Feuerbach (1804–72) was a German philosopher and student of Hegel who went on to join the Young Hegelians. His most famous work, *The Essence of Christianity*, proposed that religion is 'the dream of the human mind', in other words, man creates an illusory God based on human ideals and experiences. Feuerbach saw God as a projection of mankind's inner self and every aspect of God – morality, love, understanding, etc. – corresponds with the needs of human nature. In this way, God is not separate from man or above him. This viewpoint was derived from a development of Hegel's theory of the universal mind as discussed in the previous section of this chapter. Marx and Engels were enthusiastic about Feuerbach's theories at first but later came to reject them in *The German Ideology* and the *Theses on Feuerbach*.

How did Marx differ from those who went before?

Hegel's ideas were important but Marx did not think they went far enough. Hegel believed that civilization had reached its final stage in the Prussian Empire and that there was no need for it to progress any further; he believed the State was the most important part of society. He accepted the political development and religious views within the Prussian Empire, so he believed that in any conflict between the State and the individual the State should prevail. He also held the rather contradictory view that human consciousness could achieve self-understanding and freedom. It was these apparent contradictions that were discussed by the Young Hegelians who, as we have seen, were instrumental in shaping Marx's philosophy.

Hegel said that people felt alienated from the world around them because of religious views that mean they are striving to live in an ideal world that they can only inhabit when they die. Bauer and Feuerbach criticized religion and tried to show people that God was a creation of their own minds so that there was no need to feel alienated. Feuerbach felt that even Hegel's concept of a universal mind alienated people and that man himself was the centre of philosophy. He felt that the universal mind was a concept that prevented people from believing they could change their situation.

Where Marx differed from all these philosophers was his realization that it was not 'God' or 'Mind' that alienated people but money: 'Money is the alienated essence of man's labour and life ... it dominates him as he worships it'. It was then that he decided to devote his life to the study of economics and the way in which it affected social development. His development of historical materialism, a way of studying the ways in which the material world affects the world of ideas, came from his interest in Hegel's philosophy but his own philosophy was also greatly influenced by his study of the great British political economists.

Political economy

In a pamphlet on slavery in 1849 the writer and historian Thomas Carlyle described economics as 'the dismal science'. The study of political economy had begun to become very intense during the Industrial Revolution and was written about at length. As this revolution took place mainly in Britain, most of the great political economists were British. They were analysing and commenting on a new form of trading and business that affected the structure of society, and some of their writings, such as those of Malthus on population and Samuel Smiles on self-help, were an attempt to justify the poor treatment of the workforce.

Insight

Samuel Smiles' book, *Self-Help*, was published in 1859 and was a Victorian best seller. It stresses the importance of hard work, thrift and perseverance and implies that poverty is the fault of the individual and not of society as a whole.

When Marx started working as a journalist and writing about the problems of the wine-growers and Prussian peasants, he began to read the works of the political economists in order to understand the practical realities of a world that he had little understanding of. There were two main political economists that Marx took an interest in.

Adam Smith (1723–90) lived in Glasgow, one of the growing industrial centres in Scotland. His view of human nature was that it was natural for people to want to 'truck and barter' and so he believed the capitalist system could be justified as an extension of this natural need. In 1776 he wrote *The Wealth of Nations* which argued that government intervention in the economy would be harmful because it would destroy the natural equilibrium of the economy that he strongly believed in. Smith's ideas were an important part of the progress of political economy because he was the first to recognize that capitalists belonged to a class of their own. He also examined and described ideas of supply and demand which are now an important part of economic theory.

David Ricardo (1772–1823) wrote *The Principles of Political Economy* in 1817. He was born into a family of Sephardic Jews who had emigrated to England and he had a great deal of experience in monetary affairs as he joined his father at the London Stock Exchange at the age of 14. He did not become interested in economic theory until he read Adam Smith's *The Wealth of Nations*. This inspired him to start work on his own theories and to begin writing about them. One of his interests was the value of commodities and Marx later developed his theories into the labour theory of value (there is more detail on this in Chapter 4). Ricardo saw the capitalist society as a natural thing but identified that there would be a class struggle over the division of profits in society.

What part did Engels play?

There is no doubt that Engels was an important figure in the life of Karl Marx: 'I owe it all to you, that this has been possible',

Marx wrote in a letter to his friend. As the son of a wealthy manufacturer, Engels was able to support the Marx family financially, allowing Marx to continue with his research and writing. However, there is great academic debate over the part he played in formulating Marx's philosophy. It is difficult for us to know now how much Engels actually contributed to the body of work Marx published during his lifetime.

Marx met Engels in Paris where they became great friends and co-writers and began collaborating on *The Holy Family*. This was intended to be a pamphlet exploring the class struggle but it eventually became a 300-page book. Engels only contributed 15 pages to the total. Other works on which they collaborated were *The German Ideology*, a criticism of current German philosophy, and *The Communist Manifesto*. Again we know from documentary evidence that Marx contributed most of the writing.

It is alleged that Engels wrote newspaper articles on behalf of Marx when Marx was too busy to do his own research. He also helped with translation and as an interpreter when Marx met foreign workers' leaders. Engels wrote mainly about science, business and industrial practice, of which he had first-hand experience from his father's textile mill in Manchester. He also specialized in writing on questions of war and nationalism.

It is well known that he completed the second and third volumes of *Das Kapital* from the unfinished manuscripts and notes that Marx left behind after his death. Marx was notorious for having bad handwriting and being badly organized so it was fortunate that the business-minded and efficient Engels was available to sort everything out. How much he altered the original manuscripts or put his own interpretation on the work is open to speculation.

When Marx died Engels became *the* well-known authority on communism and tried to keep all followers to the true path. He became the interpreter of all that Marx had said or written and kept up a huge correspondence until his death in 1895.

THINGS TO REMEMBER

▶ *Marx was both a philosopher and an economist, but he believed philosophy was not enough to change the course of the world.*

▶ *He studied philosophy as far back as the ancient Greeks.*

▶ *Philosophers see the world in either idealist or materialist terms.*

▶ *Marx's view was materialist and developed from the ideas of Hegel, Bauer and Feuerbach.*

▶ *He was also greatly influenced by the works of British political economists.*

▶ *He had some dealings with revolutionaries, anarchists and Utopian Socialists but could not agree with most of their theories.*

▶ *His main contribution to the development of philosophy was historical materialism: a way of studying the relationship between the material world and the world of ideas.*

▶ *Friedrich Engels was an important figure in the life of Karl Marx but academics cannot agree on the amount he contributed to Marx's philosophy.*

4

Economic theory

In this chapter you will learn:
- *about Marx's economic analysis of capitalism*
- *how historical materialism relates to the economy*
- *key facts about labour, labour power and the division of labour*
- *about commodities, money and capital*
- *about profits and surplus value*
- *why Marx believed capitalism was in crisis.*

Marx's major work on the economy was *Das Kapital*, the writing of which took many years. Marx often believed he was nearly finished only to find something more he needed to take into account, much to the dismay of his publisher. Marx began to be interested in the workings of the economy during his time as a journalist. When writing about the plight of the peasants and the political unrest in Europe, he began a serious study of the writings of political economists such as Adam Smith and David Ricardo. Until then his learning was based around the rarefied ideas of philosophers. *Das Kapital* was the end product of a long and systematic study of both political economy and the Blue Books in which the British Government recorded factory and census statistics. The Blue Books gave Marx first-hand evidence to illustrate some of his theories.

His work on *Das Kapital* really began in 1857 in a document that is now called the *Grundrisse*. This is German for 'foundations' or 'elements' and the original document was an investigation of the basic foundations of political economy. The original document comprised notes made in preparation for *A Contribution to the Critique of Political Economy* and *Das Kapital* and was not intended for publication. Basically it was an early and rough draft of the finished work. Between these notes and the final publication of *Das Kapital* there were ten years of hard work. Marx wrote other works on the economy and economic theory around the same time, all of them stepping stones to the final work.

▶ *1845–6* – The German Ideology. *This was not published until after his death and it was a collaboration with Engels. It is important because it states the theory of the materialist view of history and further discusses alienation in a capitalist world.*

▶ *1859* – A Critique of Political Economy. *A short piece on economics that is important mainly for the preface, which summarizes the theory of historical materialism.*

▶ *1861–3* – Theories of Surplus Value *(sometimes known as* Das Kapital: *Volume 4). This work was contained in 23 huge notebooks and was not published until 1906–8. It is mainly notes for* Das Kapital *and deals with the historical perspective of economic theory.*

A whole branch of Marxist economics has flourished in academic circles and his theories go in and out of fashion. His economic theories can be interpreted in different ways: his views altered slightly through time as he developed his theories and foreign editions were slightly different from each other. Engels translated much of his work into English and simplified it for the general reader, and this is where a lot of controversy has taken place. *Das Kapital* consists of three volumes (or four if you count *Theories of Surplus Value*, extracted from Marx's notes, as a part of the whole, which some people do). There are also numerous books of notes as yet unpublished.

In Volume 1, Marx looks at the form the capitalist economy takes and explains his economic theories in great detail. The first nine chapters deal with the explanation of his economic theory; the rest of the book explores the evidence which shows the ways in which capitalists exploit their workers. Volumes 2 and 3 of *Das Kapital* were published by Engels, written by him but based on notes that Marx left before he died. Volume 2 of *Das Kapital* deals mainly with the way money is transformed into **capital** and the way in which the circulation of capital and profit combine to form an economic system.

Volume 3 deals with capitalist production as a whole and the part that competition has to play in the economy. The first volume is the most interesting one for the non-academic reader. The second and third volumes are rather more dry and of interest mainly for those with a deep and theoretical thirst for knowledge of political economics and historical materialism.

Despite being the most interesting for the lay person, the first volume is not an easy read, especially as many people today are not always aware of the literary references that Marx uses; he was rather fond of using puns and allusions to books that he was reading at the time. Also, it is rather off-putting to open a book to find that it seems to consist of 50 per cent footnotes in tiny writing (for anyone really interested in what Marx had to say, the first volume is worth reading and the footnotes are some of the most interesting sections). Fortunately, for those without the time for a marathon reading session, there are two other works that explain Marx's economic theory. As these works were based on lectures given to working men's associations they are expressed in much simpler terms, but they still explain his economic theories in great detail. They are:

▶ Wage-labour and Capital – *based on lectures given in 1847 and finally published in 1849*
▶ Value, Price and Profit – *based on lectures given in 1865 and not discovered until after Marx's death.*

Das Kapital was not written solely as a book on economics, however. It was an amalgam of history, society and economics; Marx was not interested in economics purely as a way of predicting market prices in the way Adam Smith or David Ricardo had been in their explorations of political economy. Marx was interested more in the concept of the economy and its relation to the society around him at that time in history. He wished to describe the capitalist society, to understand what had formed that society, to see how it worked and to try and predict how it would develop or be destroyed by its internal contradictions or dialectics.

Dialectical materialism, historical materialism and economy

Dialectical materialism is a term that is often used in relation to Marx and Marxist thought but it was not a phrase that Marx used himself.

Insight

It is always important to examine the source of any information and differentiate between what Marx actually said and how it has been interpreted.

It probably entered Marxist theory through the writings of Georgi Pleknanov, a Russian socialist, and became popularized as a term under the rule of Lenin in the Soviet Union. Dialectical materialism is a synthesis of the philosophical terms of dialectics and materialism. Dialectics is often used in different ways by philosophers but most of them agree that conflict, or contradiction, is a part of the development of any dialectic process.

In the last chapter we saw that Marx was greatly influenced by Hegel and by Hegel's use of the dialectic: a philosophical belief that the thesis is always contradicted by the antithesis but eventually develops into the *Aufhebung* or sublation. Hegel's dialectic view was an attempt to explain the growth and development of human history and thought; his philosophy was an idealist one, believing spirit to be at the centre of the development of history. Marx took a materialist view of the dialectic. He concentrated on the actual, material contradictions of life rather than on abstract philosophical theories and from this he developed the view that history was a product of class struggle.

Marx himself used the phrase the 'materialist conception of history' to describe his theory and Engels shortened this to the phrase 'historical materialism'. Marx saw capitalism not as the end of a process of the development of history as Hegel did, or as a natural result of the desire of people to 'truck and barter' in the way that Adam Smith did, but as a transitory phase in the progression of history. It would be a transitory state of society because of the internal contradictions or dialectics that would bring about its downfall.

This materialist view of history and its relation to economics is an important part of Marxist thought, for inherent in the dialectic viewpoint is the idea that the capitalist economy can only develop by swinging from one extreme to the other and that it will eventually collapse as a result of the contradictions present within it. In the dialectic view of the world everything is interconnected, constantly in motion and in a process of change, even society and the economy. This was what Marx was trying to understand and explain in his writing of *Das Kapital*.

The capitalist economy

In *Das Kapital* Marx described the capitalist system that he saw had developed in Europe from feudalism. At the time Marx was writing, the Industrial Revolution in Europe was changing the way that people lived and worked into a capitalist one. It is important to remember that when Marx wrote *Das Kapital*, although capitalist industry and the factory system were very important in a few countries in Europe, mainly Britain and France, most of Europe and the rest of the world were still living in a semi-feudal way. Today capitalist technology, industry and economics are on a worldwide scale, something that Marx predicted in his writing.

Marx's historical and materialist view of the world economy states that there had been four main stages in the development of the economy and society up to and including capitalism:

- **Primitive communism** – *This was the type of society of primitive hunter-gatherers where people had to work in a co-operative way to benefit from the food and raw materials provided by nature. Marx saw this form of society as a classless one.*
- **Slave society** – *This developed where some people gained power over others, usually as a result of warfare and so there was a lower class of those that worked and were not free and an upper class that exploited them.*
- **Feudalism** – *In feudalism the land was divided up between nobles in return for support for the ruler of the country. There was a strict class hierarchy from royalty at the top, down through nobles, clergy, merchants, guild artisans and serfs. The serfs had some claim to their own land but most of their labour belonged to the lord and they had to pay taxes or tithes to the nobles and the Church.*
- **Capitalism** – *This is a form of society that developed after the French Revolution, which comprised two main classes: the bourgeoisie and the proletariat. These classes are explained in more detail in Chapter 6, but basically the bourgeoisie were the rich and middle classes and the proletariat were the workers. It is also an economic system where the means of production are mostly privately owned and capital is invested in goods and services in order to make a profit. It is the dominant economic system in the Western world today, but at the time that Marx was writing it was just beginning to spread as a result of the Industrial Revolution in Europe. The word capitalism began to be used by Marxists and was popularized by them. Like many terms attributed to Marx, it was one he did not use himself. He generally used the phrase 'the capitalist mode of production' when talking in economic terms, or 'bourgeois society' when describing more social aspects.*

Marx's date for the beginning of the capitalist mode of production was the last third of the eighteenth century, for this was when industrial developments led to the factory system of manufacture. Before this the economy had been a mercantile one, based on the trading of merchants and the accumulation of wealth in the form of gold or precious metals. The agricultural system was changing too. The 'Enclosure Acts' in Britain meant that commonly owned land came under private ownership. Instead of serfs living at subsistence level on the land of a feudal lord, with some rights on common land, they began to grow cash crops for sale on the open market.

Under the feudal system, workers were tied to plots of land without rights. Their **surplus products** then became the property of an aristocratic landlord class. The capitalist system had a different economic structure because it relied on costly machinery and factories before products could be made. Only those with money to invest could afford to own these.

Capitalism is unique because:

▶ *Only under capitalism does human* **labour power** *become a* **commodity** *to be bought or sold.*
▶ *Under capitalism all production is the production of commodities.*

Commodities

The classical economist Adam Smith defined commodities as products that are produced to be sold on the market. Commodities existed before capitalism, as did money. However, under capitalism the economy is dominated by commodity production in a way that didn't exist in pre-capitalist society. In feudal or slave societies, a person would usually exchange a commodity to obtain something that they needed, and money, if it was used, was just an intermediate stage of the process. Marx showed this financial circulation as C–M–C, where C stands for the commodity and M is money. The producer would sell his commodity for money and use the money to buy another commodity that he needed.

Under capitalism the circulation is slightly more complicated and can be shown as M–C–M1. In this case the money is invested by the capitalist to produce commodities which are then exchanged for more money. In capitalism the final amount of money is greater than the initial amount that was invested and this is the profit or, as Marx called it, the 'surplus value'.

Theory of surplus value

Profit and surplus value were terms used in the works of classical economists like Smith and Ricardo but they were terms that were taken for granted and not examined in detail by them. At face value you make a profit if you sell something for more than you paid for it, but what makes one thing worth more than another, who decides it and how? Marx wanted to explore the question that puzzled the economists of the time: where does surplus value come from? To understand this he compared the way he believed the feudal economy worked with the workings of the economy under the capitalist mode of production.

Under the feudal system the landlord allowed his workers to cultivate the land in return for unpaid work, or rent, or both. It was obvious to all concerned that the landlord acquired the surplus product. Under capitalism this fact is hidden. Workers appear to be free to sell their labour power to the person who will give them the highest wages. It appears that they are given a fair day's wage for a day's work but, according to Marx, workers are being exploited. This exploitation is hidden by wages which allow the capitalist to cash in on the surplus produced by the workers. It took Marx many years to work out this **theory of surplus value**. It is a difficult concept, based on what a person's labour, or work, is actually worth and how it is exchanged for goods. To explain this it is necessary to go into detail about the way the capitalist economy works and it is more easily understood by going back to the basics of the economy as Marx did, starting with the labour theory of value.

THE LABOUR THEORY OF VALUE

All products in capitalism are commodities. According to Marx, commodities are valued in two different ways:

▶ **Use-value** – *This means a commodity has a value of 'usefulness' that meets the needs of the consumer. For example, shoes protect your feet, sugar will sweeten food, etc.*
▶ **Exchange-value** – *This refers to the relationship between the different values of different commodities; one commodity is equal to another amount of any other commodity. For example, a barrel of wine may be worth ten barrels of fish, 50 kilos of sugar or ten pairs of shoes.*

Use-values are not dependent on markets or any other system of exchange: sugar will always be useful for its sweetness. Exchange-values are dependent on market forces. A barrel of wine may be worth only nine barrels of fish one week and 11 barrels of fish the following week. In order to understand how the capitalist makes his profit Marx first of all had to understand, and explain, the rates at which goods are exchanged against each other. What is it about ten pairs of shoes that makes them worth a barrel of wine? Marx believed it was the amount of labour that went into making the product that determined the exchange-value.

Labour must be applied to any commodity to give it use-value: someone would need to catch the fish, salt them and put them in a barrel; a cobbler would have to take leather and make it into shoes. This is what Marx called **concrete labour**. Each different commodity needs a different amount of concrete labour applied to it: shoes may take ten hours to make or it may take five hours to catch and salt a barrel full of fish.

Because the commodities need to be exchanged, they must have some kind of value in common, a way of working out what they are worth against each other. Marx called what they have in common their 'value'. The value is in the commodities because they are all products of human labour. Therefore, the exchange-value of the goods can be worked out from the amount of labour that has gone into making the finished product. If a cobbler spends ten hours making shoes and a fisherman takes five hours to collect a barrel of fish then a fair rate of exchange would be two barrels of fish to one pair of shoes.

> **Insight**
>
> Marx does not take into account the concept of fashion or the more modern concern with designer labels, 'coolness', and the aesthetic aspects of consumer desire in his concept of value.

This is a very simple theory that doesn't take into account the cost of raw materials, the difficulty of the job or the skill of the worker. For example, an apprentice cobbler may take 20 hours to make a pair of shoes but this does not make the shoes more valuable. The labour theory of value depends on how much labour it takes to make a product on average or, as Marx called it, the 'socially necessary' labour time.

MONEY AND CAPITAL

In a capitalist economy goods are not usually bartered
or exchanged in this way. We use money to buy products from
the shops or markets. Money represents the value of goods and
is a useful means of exchange. Money appeared in societies that
existed before capitalism but not all money is capital. Capital is
money that is taken into circulation in order to make more
money. In Marxist terms capital is money to which surplus
value accrues.

Marx puzzled over the way in which the capitalist was able to
extract this surplus value; in other words, what is the means by
which a capitalist makes his profit? If labour is a commodity then,
like other commodities, it should be exchanged for its value. The
capitalist who employs a worker for a day should pay, on average,
the value of a day's labour, which will add the cost of a day's
labour to the cost of producing the item. Following the exchange-
value of labour theory, the capitalist can only sell or exchange the
commodity at a rate of exchange corresponding to the value of
the labour that was used to produce it. It would seem impossible
for the capitalist to make a profit, so how does he do it? Marx
worked out the solution to this problem which had puzzled many
economists before him. The answer lies in the difference between
labour and labour power.

LABOUR AND LABOUR POWER

A manufacturer of commodities needs to buy muscle power,
strength and skill from the worker in order to produce goods over
a period of time. This is labour power. It is a commodity with a
value. If the value of a commodity is the amount of labour that
goes into producing it, how much is labour power worth? Because
labour power is the strength and skill of the worker then its value
must be the value of the food, shelter, clothing, etc. that it takes to
keep the worker in a fit condition to be able to work for a specific
length of time. Labour is the actual work that is done – the activity
that adds value to raw materials.

When a capitalist hires a worker his labour power becomes labour which belongs to the capitalist. The worker is paid for his labour power at an hourly rate but what he is actually giving is his labour. There is a difference between the value of the wage which the worker receives for his labour power and the value which is created by his labour. This is the surplus value which belongs to the capitalist.

SURPLUS VALUE

Finally we get to the explanation of Marx's discovery: how the capitalist makes a profit from his workers. The capitalist pays the worker for a day's labour power and gains wealth because the worker always gets a fixed amount for his labour power regardless of the profit the capitalist makes from his labour. This is more easily understood by using an example.

If the cost of keeping a worker alive for a day is £1 and his working day is ten hours then the exchange value of ten hours labour is £10. In a factory a worker may be able to add £1 to the value of raw materials in eight hours. The worker has earned his wage in eight hours but the capitalist has bought ten hours of labour power so he is able to make a profit from the last two hours of the worker's day. This profit is multiplied by the number of workers in the factory. In effect the capitalist gets the use-value of the worker's labour power but pays only the exchange-value; the worker is getting a wage where the value is less than the value actually created by their labour. This could only occur because the capitalist economic system was unique in history: by historical and social accident the 'means of production' had come to be owned by one class, the bourgeois capitalists. This gave them the advantage over the workers who were virtually forced to sell labour on the open market in order to live. Their only alternative was to starve. In any society people have to do some kind of work in order to live, but it is only under capitalism that one class extracts surplus value in this way. In the long term this has an important relationship to the length of the working day.

Marx saw that the working day was divided into:

▶ Necessary labour – *the time the worker spends actually earning the amount paid in wages. In any society a worker would need to labour for a period of time in order to provide the food, clothing and shelter he requires. The amount of time this takes will vary according to the technology that is available to help him with his work.*
▶ Surplus labour – *the time spent producing surplus value for the capitalist.*

The capitalist can increase his surplus value by:

▶ *making the working day longer*
▶ *increasing efficiency in the workplace so the worker covers the cost of his wages in a shorter time leaving more of the rest of the day available to produce surplus value.*

Profit and the division of labour

The chief driving force in capitalism is profit. Not all the surplus value the capitalist gains from his workers is profit because he has had to pay for machinery, training, etc. The rate of profit the capitalist receives is variable and he is always looking for ways to improve it.

The capitalist system differs from past production methods by using a way of working called the division of labour. This is the use of mass production systems within the workplace so that a process is split into a number of repetitive tasks. Our old friend the cobbler would have taken the leather through every process until he finished with a pair of shoes. In a factory machines do the work in a number of different stages. One machine cuts the leather, one sews it, one shapes it, etc. This improves the capitalist's profits:

▶ *One worker can do the work of several others. This will increase competition for jobs, so wages go down.*

- *It makes the work simple and unskilled so there is no need for long apprenticeships or training.*
- *Small-scale capitalists are put out of business because they cannot compete with the low prices of the large-scale manufacturers. They then have to join the workers.*

However, this increased profit can only be gained in the short term. Once the capitalist's more efficient and improved production methods have spread to other manufacturers there will be an abundance of his product on the market. This is known as over-production and competition in the marketplace will eventually reduce the price of his commodity.

The capitalist can solve his problem in the short term by:

- *exploiting old markets more efficiently, for example by advertising*
- *opening up new markets, for example by exporting to other countries.*

Marx noted that there is always a tendency for the rate of profit to fall. Increased competition is one of the main factors in this because the capitalist finds he has to invest increasing amounts of capital into his business.

Insight

Following Marx's model it was generally believed that all modern economic crises would be as the result of over-production, but the global recession that began in 2007 included factors such as banking, investments and housing markets.

Capitalism in crisis

Marx believed that the capitalist structure of society would inevitably lead to crisis and internal contradictions would eventually lead to its downfall. The main problems that Marx predicted were:

- ▶ *Worker's wages will tend to fall to subsistence level.*
- ▶ *Profits will tend to fall.*
- ▶ *Competition will lead to large companies swallowing up small ones; this would be opposed by growing numbers of workers.*
- ▶ *More people will be forced into the working class.*
- ▶ *The capitalist system will lead to greater divisions in society.*
- ▶ *There will be more and more severe economic crises.*
- ▶ *Capitalism will reduce workers to a degraded condition and these workers will eventually rise up in revolution and overthrow the system.*

Falling wages and profits

Marx was convinced that capitalism was in crisis. Underpinning this belief was his faith in his dialectical analysis of the economy. He saw the whole of capitalism as inherently unstable because of the dialectical oppositions that make up its structure. If there was an economic 'boom' it was certain to be followed by a 'bust' or depression. He was also convinced that wages would become lower and lower until they reached subsistence level and that profits would keep falling because in capitalism the price of goods, and the profits made, are dependent to a great extent on the markets and on wages:

- ▶ *High wages for workers lead to high prices for commodities, therefore factory owners get low profits.*
- ▶ *Low wages for workers mean that they are unable to buy enough goods and services to keep the economy viable and this leads to unemployment.*

The economist John Maynard Keynes (1883–1946) made famous one of the internal paradoxes of capitalism that Marx had already pointed out. Each capitalist wants his workers to have low wages so that he can increase his profits, but he wants the workers who work for someone else to have high wages, so that they can buy his products. There is no way that this can happen in the real world and the contradictory desires of the capitalists are part of the dialectical paradox that makes the capitalist system unstable and can lead to recurring economic crises.

> **Insight**
>
> Balancing these two opposing forces is an important factor in recovery after any economic crisis. Is it better to make wages higher to increase spending and risk inflation? Or should wages be kept low because of the pressures of global competition?

Social labour

Another problem affecting profits in a capitalist society is that nobody decides who is going to make what. We saw that use-value is an important part of Marx's economic theory. The products made have to be 'useful' for some human need. But they also have to be useful for some specific need, in a specific place: for example, if you are hungry you cannot eat a pair of shoes. In order for society to function we need all different kinds of commodities. If everyone decides to make shoes, for example, we will all go hungry. So societies need to have some way of regulating who makes what to ensure that enough of the right kinds of commodities are made.

Marx called this **social production** and he pointed out that the capitalist system was unlike slave or feudal societies in this respect as there is no way of making sure this happens. To a great extent, in slave or feudal societies the slave owner or the landowner decided the distribution of labour. They decided what they wanted and who would make it so that it met their needs. In a feudal society, with rural industry, the families who made up the society further regulated the distribution of labour. Some members would grow grain, some would weave, some would make shoes and the labour would be distributed so that it was relevant to age, sex, the seasons of the year, etc. They would be producing commodities that they needed and that they had to provide specifically for those above them in the ruling classes.

Capitalism, however, is a system of **generalized commodity production**. Factories are specialized and tend to produce only one kind of product. No producer can meet all his needs from the products of his own factory so he has to sell them as commodities to other people. In this way commodity producers are interdependent on each other.

Because there is no system of regulating who makes what, apart from market forces, this can lead to problems:

▶ *It is not possible to tell if the products will be 'useful' until they go onto the market. The producer might not be able to sell them. In that case, according to Marx, the labour that has* *gone into such products is therefore not **social labour** because it has been wasted. The goods are of no use to society.*

▶ *Manufacturers often compete for the same markets by making very similar products. The most successful will be those who can make them the most cheaply. Manufacturers can only do this effectively by increasing productivity and undercutting one another.*

Insight

In Western economies markets are usually left to find their own level, but certain types of large manufacturing industries may be encouraged by government grants in order to avoid unemployment during an economic downturn.

Manufacturers do not know whether or not their products will fill a social need in advance and can only determine this by trying to sell them. Because they are interdependent on each other and in competition at the same time this must lead to market fluctuations.

We saw earlier in the chapter that the price of commodities depends on the amount of 'socially necessary' labour time that goes into making them. In the marketplace of generalized commodity production it is difficult to see how much socially necessary labour time goes into making a product. To take the example used earlier, there is no easy way of telling that a fair rate of exchange of products is two barrels of fish to one pair of shoes. Competition between manufacturers and the way that surplus value is extracted means that labour has become **abstract social labour** and related to money. This is related to the 'fetishism of commodities', which is discussed in the next chapter.

Accumulation and crisis

We have seen that in a capitalist economy surplus value is acquired from the workers and becomes profit. This is not often used by the capitalist to buy another product but is invested in further production. So surplus value goes into producing more surplus value. Marx called this the **accumulation of capital** and he believed it became almost an obsession for the capitalist. He said the bourgeois class often denied themselves their own consumption in order to invest capital, but he did not believe they were misers, hoarding their wealth just for the sake of it. He believed they were cogs in the machine of competition for they had to reinvest or be overtaken by their rivals.

Marx realized that investment of capital is important to the growth of the economy; capitalists have to plough back parts of their profit into the economy otherwise it will stagnate. However, as the markets are not controlled in any way, if the capitalist cannot sell his product because there is no demand, or if supply exceeds demand, there will be a slump. In this case people do tend to hoard their money rather than reinvest it because profits become very low. This makes the slump even greater. Large amounts of commodities remain unsold and so the capitalist does not get a profit from his investment. This is a crisis of over-production, which Marx said was unique to capitalism. Under the feudal system economic crises were usually the result of not enough being produced, leading to famine.

Centralization of the economy

Because Marx saw the competition between rival capitalists as one of the main economic problems, he believed that the economy should be managed centrally:

- *Important industries should be centralized, only useful goods and services should be produced and over-production should stop.*
- *Banks should be centralized. It is only in this way that society can be sure there are high levels of investment in the right kind of industries.*
- *There should be controls on imports to help combat unemployment.*

Marx believed that these measures could only work in the communist society that would inevitably come about as a result of inconsistencies within the capitalist system. Marx's view was in contrast to the views of Adam Smith who had a **laissez-faire** attitude to the economy. He believed that there was some 'invisible hand' that guided the markets and that pursuit of individual interests in the free market tends to regulate the economy for the greater social good. He thought it is better to leave the economy to its own devices than use any interventionist policies. Naturally, bourgeois society tended to agree with his views.

Was Marx right about the economy?

There is no doubt that capitalism has gone through repeated crises since it began. There was the 'Long Depression' in the 1870s and 1880s, and the Great Depression of the 1930s affected most of the capitalist world, increasing fears that a worldwide communist revolution was about to begin. After a relative boom period there was a series of crises beginning in the 1970s, largely as a result of fluctuations in the price of oil. At the beginning of the twenty-first century there was a world economic boom, followed by a global financial crisis beginning in 2007. More crises are predicted, but how much these are a result of the dialectic flaws inherent in capitalism is open to debate.

Modern neo-classical economists, such as those academics who follow the ideas of the **Chicago School,** would argue that boom and bust in the economy are just a part of the natural cycle of the economy. They reject the idea of dialectical instability and believe that market economies are inherently stable if left to their own devices. They believe that government intervention is the cause of depressions. They do not agree with Marx's labour theory of value, believing that value is a subjective thing that varies for different people and even for the same person at different times. They also believe that Marx's view of the economy was over-simplified and that no economic system is ever a purely capitalist one in which one group holds the means of production and one group provides the labour. They disagree with the assertion that labour is the only source of value in the economy and the only way of making a profit. They also assert that it was not market forces that caused the world financial crisis in 2007 but de-regulation of banking services and dishonest dealing in world financial markets, allied to a downturn in the US housing markets. Radical Marxists view these arguments with suspicion and say that as the present dominant view of the economic system in the West is a neo-classical one, stressing free enterprise, then it is in the interests of economists to support a system that benefits them. They also believe that although the cause of the 2007 global financial crisis was laid at the door of world banks and financiers it was only a short-term cause. The real cause is the inherent weakness of capitalism itself.

There is also much debate about whether profits and wages have fallen in the way that Marx predicted. In real terms, most people in the West are better off than they were in Marx's time, and incomes are said to be evening out. Even in developing countries there seems to be evidence of improvements in infant mortality rates and production of food supplies, which are used as indicators of poverty. Rather than the majority of people being forced into the working classes, the gap between rich and poor is being filled by a larger and wealthier middle class, but rich and poor still exist.

Marx never finished his work on the economy. Volume 1 of *Das Kapital* was the only volume he completed so he did not really have time to formulate his theories properly before his death. Because Marx's views changed throughout his lifetime, there is a lot of discussion about which of his writings should be taken into account when stating his view of the economy. Marx's theories can be used selectively to support different arguments. For example, a government that wishes to intervene in the economy could select those parts of his work where intervention is stressed and other writings ignored. Some Marxists also believe that the dialectic view of the economy has been over-stressed by previous writers because it was over-emphasized by Engels and by communist leaders who wanted to gain control over the economy.

The predictions that Marx made about the economy have not all come about: profits do not tend to fall, worker's wages have improved in real terms and the majority of people are much better off than they were in Marx's day. For the majority of people in society, class divisions have become less distinct. Where communists have come to power through revolutions their economies have suffered just as many economic crises as capitalist countries, although for different reasons. However, we have seen the takeover of smaller companies by larger ones and several depressions in the economy with periods of high unemployment, so Marx was not totally wrong, and although economists try to predict the future of the economy, they cannot really know what will happen next.

THINGS TO REMEMBER

▶ *Marx explained his economic theory in* Das Kapital. *It is also explained in* Wage-labour and Capital *and in* Value, Price and Profit.

▶ *The capitalist economy needs costly machinery to produce goods. Only those who can afford to invest capital in the economy can profit from it.*

▶ *All production under capitalism is the production of commodities.*

▶ *Human labour power becomes a commodity under capitalism.*

▶ *Marx believed workers are exploited by capitalism but they are not aware of it.*

▶ *Commodities have two types of value: use-value and exchange-value.*

▶ *The rate at which commodities are exchanged against each other depends on the amount of labour that has gone into making them.*

▶ *In a capitalist society, money is used as an indirect way of exchanging goods. Not all money is capital. Capital is money to which surplus value accrues.*

▶ *Capitalists gain surplus value from their workers by paying them a fixed amount for their labour power regardless of the profit they gain.*

▶ *Surplus value can be increased by lengthening the working day or increasing productivity.*

▶ *Not all surplus value is profit.*

- *Division of labour increases profit in the short term.*

- *Profits fall in the long term due to over-production and increased competition, which leads to increasing investment.*

- *Marx believed capitalism was in crisis and this would eventually lead to revolution.*

- *Marx believed that under communism the economy should be managed centrally.*

- *Not all of Marx's economic predictions have occurred and not all of his theories are accepted today.*

5

Economy and society

In this chapter you will learn:
- *how Marx believed the economy affected society*
- *about colonialism and imperialism*
- *about fetishism, alienation and exploitation*
- *how realization of these would lead to revolution.*

For Marx economics did not exist in a vacuum, as a subject to be studied for its own sake. He was interested in the way that the economic structure of society affected the lives of the people within it. Capitalist society had developed fairly gradually in Europe, but in the second half of the nineteenth century it had started to develop very rapidly along with technological change. Marx saw that this had very definite effects on the lives of both rich and poor. He also saw that the effects of a capitalist economy were starting to be felt around the world and not just in the countries which had developed their means of production.

Imperialism and colonialism

Marx did not publish any theory of **imperialism**, although he did make reference to **colonialism** in the first volume of *Das Kapital*. Imperialism and colonialism are sometimes used inter-changeably as words to explain the policy of one country extending control or authority over other countries outside its own borders. Colonialism is usually seen as rule over colonies that 'belong' in some way to the ruling power, for whatever reason. For example, India was at one time a British colony.

Marxists today use the term imperialism in a slightly different way from that used in a historical sense. The generally understood term describes imperialism as a policy of extending authority over foreign countries by acquiring and maintaining empires. Marxists see imperialism as the state of capitalism that takes place when colonialism has taken over the world.

This definition of imperialism comes mainly from Lenin's work *Imperialism: The Highest Stage of Capitalism*. Here he states that once all underdeveloped counties have become colonies of more developed ones there will be no new colonies available to be acquired by the major powers, unless they take them from each other. He also claims that capital will be concentrated in the 'financial oligarchy'; banking and finance will be dominant over industrial capital.

Insight

It is interesting to note Lenin's prediction in the light of the world financial crisis or global meltdown that began in 2007. This was largely attributed to a lack of regulation in the financial sector.

Imperialism is also a term much used by modern Marxists to describe the capitalist system of trade and banking and it is often used as a disparaging term to describe a greater power acting at the expense of a lesser power, regardless of whether or not the greater power has any rule over the lesser power. For example, the United States is sometimes referred to as the 'American Empire' because it is the dominant economic and military power in the world, even though it does not possess an actual physical empire.

What all these definitions of imperialism have in common is that some form of exploitation is taking place. Imperialists are often criticized for economic exploitation. The dominating power often makes use of other countries as sources of cheap labour and raw materials and as markets for manufactured goods they have produced. The concept of imperialism amounting to exploitation can be traced back to Marx's original thinking on the subject of colonialism.

Marx was ideally placed to observe and comment on the way that the British ran their colonies, for he wrote *Das Kapital* in London – one of the great centres of world trade at the heart of the Victorian British Empire. There was a saying that 'the sun never sets on the British Empire'; this was because it covered so many countries in the major continents that it straddled the world's time zones. At one time the British Empire was so vast that it contained the North American continent (including Canada), Australia and large parts of Asia and Africa. The empire had almost died out in the early nineteenth century until industrialization gave it a new lease of life.

Historians divide imperialism into periods of time or epochs:

▶ Mercantile capitalism – *This is the first stage of imperialism. It began in the sixteenth century when explorers discovered new continents and plundered them. Large companies became the governing power in countries where they settled.*
▶ Colonialism – *This is the second stage of imperialism. Capitalist countries took over governing power from the companies set up under mercantile capitalism. Where the local population would not accept this rule, armed force was used.*

Marx and Engels wrote a good deal about the position of the British in relation to one of their most profitable colonies, India. Between 1857 and 1858 they regularly wrote articles in the *New York Tribune* on the subject of colonialism in India and the dominance of the East India Company. This company played a very successful part in the annexing of the Indian subcontinent on behalf of the British Empire. It had started as a company with a monopoly in India, by virtue of a royal charter, but soon changed from being purely a trading company to ruling India with the help of a large private army. After the Indian mutiny of 1858 its territorial holdings became the property of the British crown. Marx believed that British rule in India had destroyed the Indian communal village system in a greedy and destructive manner, but although he acknowledged that the way it was done was wrong he felt that the British had inadvertently brought about progress. This was not because he believed capitalism was superior to the former system but because he believed it was only a stage on the way to a society where classes were completely abolished.

Marx saw the globalization of capitalism as inevitable. He wrote in the *Grundrisse*, 'The tendency to create the world market is directly given in the concept of capital itself'. He believed profits under capitalism would fall and that one short-term way of slowing down the rate at which profits fell was by opening up new markets. This meant the capitalists had to export their goods into other countries. Colonialism meant there were excellent protected markets for manufactured goods. Even where former colonies became self-governing countries, such as Australia, they often had economic and trade agreements that meant they were still dependent on Britain.

In the early nineteenth century Britain was really the only fully industrialized nation and was known as 'the workshop of the world' as it produced about 30 per cent of global industrial output. By the end of the nineteenth century other European states and the USA were able to enter the world of capitalist exporters. They made things very efficiently and flooded the world markets with cheap goods, which meant they could undercut any of the opposition. The markets for these cheap goods were often developed at the expense of local industries. Historians believe millions of villagers died of starvation in India because their traditional textile industry was ruined by imports of cheap manufactured cotton from Lancashire. India and other countries were turned into suppliers of cheap raw materials for British industry.

Capitalism could not develop in these countries in the early stages
of their exploitation as they were deliberately held back from
any form of development. It was only later, at the beginning of
the twentieth century, that the capitalist system itself began to be
exported. There was investment in the employment of industrial
workers in the colonies, but only when this did not interfere with
industries in Britain and the other imperialist states. This was
mainly in industries that were fairly close to the raw materials:
mining, food processing, etc. At this stage in history there was
also a huge scramble for power between European nations in
the African continent. Some modern Marxists believe these factors
led the way to the growth of the **developing world** and the current
stage of imperialism: neo-colonialism.

Marx believed that revolution would only take place on a
worldwide scale after the capitalist system had been exported.
He was convinced that revolution could only take place if societies
had developed to the stage of capitalism with the class divisions
of bourgeois and proletariat, for it was the proletariat who
would start the revolution. The revolutionary process would
have two stages:

▶ *Firstly, there would be a bourgeois revolution against
  imperialism.*
▶ *Secondly, there would be a revolution of the proletariat against
  the bourgeoisie.*

Marx was not a trained economist and although globalization of
the capitalist system did occur it was not entirely in the way that he
predicted. He saw the world economic situation in a rather simple
way and in reality the colonies had very different social structures
that he did not entirely take into account. Their developing
economies were combinations of widely different economic
systems; very few were entirely capitalist in nature.

Communist revolutions did take place in some former colonies, but Marx's words were often distorted to fit the requirements of anybody who wished to see a change in the political system in their country. A truly communist society, without classes, was never the result.

Insight

An example of a former colony that came under communist rule is North Vietnam, which was part of French Indo–China. This ultimately led to the Vietnam War of 1959–1975.

Fetishism

In primitive societies, and in some kinds of religion, inanimate objects are sometimes thought to have supernatural powers (for example, voodoo dolls or holy statues). In capitalist societies people suffer from the illusion that inanimate money or commodities also have powers and properties of their own. A fetish is an object of desire, worship or obsessive concern. Marx saw three types of **fetishism** in capitalist society:

- ▶ *fetishism of money*
- ▶ *fetishism of capital*
- ▶ *fetishism of commodities.*

MONEY FETISHISM

Throughout history money has always had an element of fetishism about it, especially when it was in the form of precious metals, gold in particular. Seventeenth and eighteenth century European merchants were obsessed with gold and silver and believed that possession of large quantities of precious metals would be enough to let a country win a war. However, gold in itself is worthless. If you have ever read the book *Treasure Island* by R. L. Stevenson you will remember the character Ben Gunn, who was marooned on a desert island with a treasure chest. The treasure was of no use to

him because he could not use it to buy anything and what he really desired was a little bit of cheese. Money fetishism is an illusion that deceives workers, making them think of money as the goal of their labours and thinking of their worth in terms of money.

CAPITAL FETISHISM

This is the belief that capital in itself is valuable and that it does not owe anything to the labour that goes to produce it. Marx argued that capitalists felt that increased productivity was due to the capital they invested in their business and not the labour of the workers. Capitalists also feel that their money is productive when it is in a bank earning interest. Although it is making them a profit, it is not actually producing anything.

COMMODITY FETISHISM

One of the great points of controversy among Marxists and academics is the idea of commodity fetishism. This is possibly because Marx did not write very clearly on the subject and the idea seems a rather abstract one. At one level Marx seems to be saying that because the capitalist is exploiting the worker there is a hidden aspect to the real value of a commodity that nobody is aware of, that there is a veil of secrecy over the true worth of the products we buy. A modern-day example of this would be 'designer labels', where goods that are produced cheaply in countries in the developing world sell at vastly inflated prices because of some false idea of their worth. It is very difficult for the buyer to know what the materials cost, who made them, how much the workers were paid, etc.

At another level is the belief that some commodities have a kind of intrinsic value that makes them more valuable than others and is not related to their exchange-value. For example, some commodities, such as holy statues, appear to have magical properties that make us blind as to their real value and so we become alienated. This is a more difficult argument to understand and some Marxist critics believe it is an interpretation that Marx did not intend in his original writing. Whatever interpretation is placed on the idea of fetishism, it is clear that Marx believed that under capitalism people experience social relations as value relations between things and that this causes alienation. We can take the example of the pair of shoes again and look at the idea in a less abstract way. A woman might desire an expensive pair of shoes she sees in a shop and will work to have enough money to buy those shoes. In a capitalist society the money and shoes are independent from each other in a social sense. The people who made the shoes and the woman buying them are not aware of each other or of any social relationship between them. Marx believed that this caused alienation in society, because we are not in immediate relation to the products we buy. This then leads to a vicious circle where people believe they can relieve the alienation they feel by buying more consumer items.

The idea of commodity fetishism is strongly reliant on the labour theory of value and the concepts of exploitation and alienation, so critics of those concepts criticize fetishism as well. Marx believed that all three kinds of fetishism were features of capitalist society that stopped people from understanding and changing the society. They are illusions that play a part in the alienation of humans under capitalism.

ALIENATION

Marx wrote a great deal about alienation and it is one of the areas of his thought that is still acknowledged as having great relevance today. Most of us are familiar with the term 'alienation' today: a sense of feeling outside society or estranged from it. Following on from this is the feeling that life has become worthless, pointless or not worth living.

The Marxist sense of alienation is more complex than this. For Marx alienation is not just a feeling or philosophical concept but an actual, concrete thing: a state of being that is a result of living in a capitalist society. To understand this we need to look at the way Marx views humanity and society.

Marx developed his theory of alienation throughout most of his lifetime, beginning with some original notes that he made in the *Economic and Philosophical Manuscripts of 1844*. These are incomplete, and in *Das Kapital*, written much later in his life, the idea of alienation was transformed into the idea of fetishism. This has led to much discussion as to what Marx really meant by alienation and whether his early work should be taken into account; however, this early work is integral to the understanding of the Marxist concept of alienation.

Insight

The *Economic and Philosophical Manuscripts of 1844* are also known as the *Paris Manuscripts* because Marx wrote them while living there, although they were not published until after his death.

In the incomplete fragment '*Alienated Labour*', a part of the *Manuscripts of 1844*, Marx appears to be trying to formulate a complete theory of alienation that would encompass all the different ways that the capitalist society alienates its members. He was trying to find some unifying and underlying cause. In his later work he abandons the attempt at an overriding theory, but alienation is still a large part of his thought.

Most of Marx's early work shows a great debt to Hegel and his theory of alienation, which can be traced from the philosophy of Hegel and its development by Feuerbach. Hegel had shown that people were alienated but believed it was due to their yearning to be part of the universal mind. Alienation for him was a religious concept. People naturally yearn to have what they perceive as a unifying and spiritual essence within themselves. Most religions (and we have to remember that Hegel was talking mainly about Western religion) say this can only be achieved by a supernatural being that lives outside the real world, and the only way humans can achieve this is by merging with this being at some level, usually after death. Hegel believed this led to a kind of **false consciousness** where people believe they are separate from the divine or opposed to it in some way. They are estranged or alienated from spirituality. This then leads to alienation in the sense of feeling worthless because they feel that the real world around them is no substitute for this divine experience. Their lives are spent in trying to reconcile the human spirit with the divine one and so they become estranged from the real and natural world.

Feuerbach saw alienation in less mystical terms for he believed that 'God' was not outside us but a product of the human mind. The values we attribute to God are those that we ourselves possess but we project them onto God. In this way, we become alienated from ourselves. This means that we are separated from our own true essence and from each other. Feuerbach believed that if people could free themselves from religious illusion then they would be able to live in harmony with each other and with their own true nature.

Marx saw alienation in practical, economic terms and for him it is not even necessary for a person to feel alienated to be alienated, it comes as a result of living in a capitalist society. In order to understand why he believed this we need to look at the way Marx perceived the human condition. Marx did not see human nature as an abstract and unchanging thing as the philosophers before him had done. After studying the economics of society in historical context he saw human nature as a product of social relations. His historical materialism gave him the view that human nature is in a constant process of development, and that as societies change so do the needs of the people in them. That does not mean that he saw human nature as a totally abstract concept, as has been argued by some writers. Marx saw that there was some underlying common ground about the nature of humanity in all societies, despite the differences in politics and economic systems. In his writings he talks of the 'species being' which is the essence of humanity and a development of the ideas of Feuerbach. Feuerbach believed that the true essence of humanity was the love and harmony that brought people together in society.

Marx, on the other hand, believed that 'labour is the essence of man' and that people are labouring creatures; humans are basically producers and being able to work in purposeful creative activity brings us contentment. In this way we might be seen to be similar to ants or bees, but for Marx we differ greatly from them because we possess consciousness. Marx saw that humans, like animals, are a part of nature; we have similar needs for food, shelter and a desire to reproduce our species, but our consciousness means we are aware of what we are doing. We are aware of who we are and we see ourselves in relation to the rest of our species. This is important, for unless we are conscious of these things in the first place we cannot feel alienated from them. In fact some **existentialist** philosophers would maintain that is precisely because we are self-conscious that we feel alienated; they argue that it is part of the human condition and it would not matter what kind of society we lived in. Marx did not believe it was only consciousness that distinguishes us from animals and he develops this idea in *The German Ideology*. Here he writes that is not just consciousness or religion that distinguishes us from animals but that human beings differentiate themselves from animals as soon as they begin to produce their 'means of subsistence'. Meaningful work is important to all humans. For Marx, labour is an important part of social development and fundamental to human beings, for through it we change nature and society and in the process we change our selves.

The opposite of alienation is actualization, or affirmation of the self, which Marx believed humans achieved from the purposeful use of their consciousness. He did not believe that work was supposed to be drudgery to be done away with, as many of the Utopian Socialists believed. Work is an integral part of humanity and unless people are in right relation to it then they will be alienated; according to Marx, labour is essential to the 'species being' of man but the new capitalist system changed the ways that people worked so that they were not in a 'right relation' to their labour. The factory system, and the society that had grown up around that, had perverted the natural relations of people to the products of their labour and to each other.

The capitalist system of working alienates all those in it, both rich and poor. Workers are alienated from the products they make because they do not benefit from them. They see the products of their labours as 'alien and outside them'. 'Labour produces fabulous things for the rich but misery for the poor', Marx wrote in the *Economic and Philosophic Manuscripts*.

Workers are alienated and depersonalized by the capitalist system because of the way in which the capitalist obtains surplus value from their labour. The capitalist system also means that they are told when to work, how to work and they derive very little personal satisfaction from their labours.

The environment of some parts of the capitalist system, the factory system, is dehumanizing: it is hostile to the workers and physically and mentally damaging to them. The constant repetitive nature of the work is not harmonious with human nature. The division of labour and the way the factory system is set up is also not natural, according to Marx, because it encourages competition instead of co-operation and it alienates people from each other.

Exploitation

Alienation is connected to exploitation by the capitalist. Marx saw the exploitation of one class by another as a fundamental part of an industrialized capitalist society. Marx believed that there had always been exploitation but it was only under the capitalist system that exploiting others became the normal way of working. In Chapter 4 we saw that the capitalists hold the balance of power. They are able to make a profit from the surplus value because they own the means of production. The worker is not aware of the fact that he is being exploited. He believes the capitalist has a right to the surplus value that is produced because he believes that is just the way things are, or part of human nature. This kind of exploitation is not really visible, unlike the more common forms of exploitation such as making people work long hours, child labour and difficult and dangerous working practices and conditions.

In the introduction to *Das Kapital* Marx says that he has not painted a picture of capitalists and landlords in a 'rosy light'. There are many examples of explicit exploitation of workers given as examples in the book. Chapter 10, The Working Day, consists of mountains of evidence that Marx collected from reports and newspaper articles. Evidence includes children working in mines and heavy industry in appalling conditions, engine drivers working 21-hour shifts, and dressmakers and milliners forced to work in overcrowded sweatshops where they died of consumption. Capital is 'vampire like', writes Marx in the introduction, and it 'sucks living labour'.

In the Victorian era the average age for death among the working classes was just 19 years. Marx records descriptions of the physical state of many of the workers in British industrial cities in *Das Kapital*; many of the examining doctors report on the undernourished and progressively stunted growth of the working classes.

Marx believed that a shorter working day would greatly benefit those people and in most democratic countries today there are laws to regulate the hours that people have to work. The workers who had to fight for improvements in working conditions by uniting against the capitalists found their inspiration in the works of Marx.

Marx did not make overt moral judgements on the capitalists; he tried to distance himself from any moral commentary in his writing and tried to keep true to the idea of objective materialism. He saw *Das Kapital* as a scientific study. However, anyone who writes in such an emotive way as Marx does, comparing capitalists to 'werewolves' and 'vampires' (as he does in *Das Kapital*) is obviously not in favour of capitalism as a system and is making a moral statement. Marx applauded those who did their best to alleviate working conditions but he believed that both worker and capitalist alike are victims of the system. The capitalist is only a part of the society around him and has no choice but to continue with things the way they are, for even if a factory owner were to give away his goods and his factory somebody else would take his place. In the *Grundrisse* Marx appears to disagree with the Romantic ideal that believes life was better in some pre-capitalist rural idyll. He saw capitalism as a great civilizing influence but believed it was only a part of the progression of history and not the final stage of development as others at the time believed. Marx thought that it would give way to communism and that it is only under a communist system that there would be no exploitation of any kind. He believed this society would only come about when people become aware of the true nature of society and their alienation.

Marx believed that capitalism seduces consumers by giving them desires which enslave them. The goods that a worker produces eventually enslave him because he is trapped in a cycle of working for money to buy goods; fetishism of goods means that people want to buy and consume more. The fetishism of money means that people have to sell themselves to obtain it and then desire money for its own sake. Private property also alienates people because they believe that an object only has worth if they can possess or use it. Marx even went so far as to say that people do not appreciate objects for their aesthetic beauty but only in relation to their commercial value.

Private property, wage labour, surplus value, and market forces are structures that have been constructed by people in society. These structures manipulate everyone in society but in subtle ways so they don't realize what is happening. Because people are not aware of the way in which they are manipulated by the economy they feel alienated and do not know why. Marx believed that even capitalists are alienated but they are 'happy in their alienation'. Their power, wealth and privilege are substitutes for true happiness.

On the other hand, the alienation of the workers is oppressive. They are the ones who truly suffer from alienation as they have nothing – neither the means of production nor the end products. All they hold is their labour power. The capitalist cannot exist without the worker; the worker believes he cannot survive without the capitalist because of the hold that money and wage labour have over him. In *The German Ideology* Marx describes how the abolition of private property and regulation of labour would abolish alienation between them and their products and would let them be in control of their lives again. Marx believed that realization of alienation was a vital step towards the revolution that would bring about communism. Capitalism was in crisis due to its internal conflicts, and it would go through a series of crises that would bring it to its knees. Once the workers understood their alienation and exploitation they would rise up and help to finish it off. A revolution would take place.

THINGS TO REMEMBER

▶ *Marx was interested in the ways in which the economy affected society.*

▶ *Capitalism spread around the world through imperialism.*

▶ *Communism could also spread around the world, but colonies would only be ready for revolution after industrialization had taken place.*

▶ *Marx described how fetishism of money, capital and commodities alienated people.*

▶ *Alienation is connected to exploitation.*

▶ *People are alienated by a society that they have constructed but they don't realize this.*

▶ *Workers are oppressed by their alienation because they do not own the means of production.*

▶ *Capitalists are alienated but are happy in their alienation because they have material possessions.*

▶ *Realization of alienation would lead to class struggle and revolution.*

6

Class, class struggle and revolution

In this chapter you will learn:

- *how Marx defined class*
- *how capitalist society developed*
- *about ideology and false consciousness*
- *about workers' power and organization*
- *how class consciousness could lead to revolution.*

Introduction

Long before Marx, historians had discovered the existence of social classes, but class awareness and classification became more important in Europe at the end of the eighteenth century as a result of the French Revolution. Adam Smith was one of the first English writers to look at class, in an economic sense, in *The Wealth of the Nations*: here he describes class conflict between 'masters' and 'labourers'. Today there are many ways of defining class in society. Sociologists might see class as defined by the functions of people in a society, for example managerial workers, white-collar workers, blue-collar workers, etc. or they may define class according to income or by cultural tastes and habits.

Marx did not define class in any of his works and used the term rather loosely to mean different things at different times but he believed that class is defined purely by economic factors. He saw that classes are made up of individuals who share a common relationship with the means of production. At the time he was writing, he saw that the capitalist economy had divided society into two opposing camps: 'two great classes opposing each other: Bourgeoisie and Proletariat'. Those who owned the means of production were the bourgeoisie, those who owned no means of production were the proletariat.

Insight

Modern definitions of class are much broader than Marx's definition and society can be seen to be structured in different ways depending on whether you are studying social issues, looking at economic factors, or doing market research.

Marx wanted to understand how this situation had come about and spent many years studying the development of the capitalist system that had grown up in Europe after the Industrial Revolution. He believed a scientific study of the ways in which society had developed would help prepare the working classes to overthrow the system by showing them the historical perspective of their position. He believed that capitalism was the latest form of exploitation in a series of oppressive rules throughout history and that if people were shown this then they could be persuaded to take action against their oppressors. It was only in this way that a classless communist society would eventually come about.

The development of capitalist society

In the earliest societies, when people lived as hunter-gatherers and small-scale farmers, there were no real classes as society was organized on the basis of common labour and mutual protection and there was no private property. People scratched out an existence at subsistence level and had just enough food for basic survival. In Marxist theory this type of society is known as 'primitive communism'.

As societies became more efficient in producing food, the surplus products often came under the control of a ruling elite. The surplus products allowed the ruling elite to live off the labour of those below them in the class structure without having to produce anything themselves. This elite was often only a minority of the society as a whole. Throughout history the ruling elite has changed: slave owners, religious leaders of many types, feudal lords and, finally, capitalists.

In *The Communist Manifesto*, Marx and Engels defined capitalists as the owners of the means of production and the employers of wage labourers. Because the factory system that sprang up after the Industrial Revolution was based on the purchase of large items of machinery, it was only a minority of the population who could afford to invest in it, so they became the new ruling elite.

Dialectical materialism and class structure

Marx saw history as a series of dialectical conflicts. Each type of society, whether based on slavery, feudalism or capitalism, contains contradictions inside its structure which can only be expressed through conflict. These conflicts eventually lead to the downfall of the system. A new system then takes its place. Marx said this had been demonstrated throughout history.

In the original hunter-gatherer societies there was no real division of labour; everybody could do any job that needed to be done and could use any of the tools that were available. These societies were classless in a Marxist sense, but then they developed into slave-owning societies which became unstable and collapsed due to internal contradictions. The ownership of slaves was dependent on warfare, which put pressure on the economy. Eventually, this undermined the power of the state, allowing barbarian invasion, which then led to the collapse of the system.

Feudalism replaced slavery in Europe and it allowed people to develop skills and talents under the patronage of the landed nobility. However, feudalism was eventually overthrown by revolutionary struggles which continued into the nineteenth century when the rise of capitalism began.

Capitalism was necessary to allow the development of the factory system and mass production. People had to be legally free to move to where the work was, instead of being tied to the land. The landowners also had to be legally free to accumulate wealth and to be able to invest it to make a profit.

According to Marx, no social system has appeared accidentally, but when it was historically necessary. Each new system outlives its usefulness. Within every process, internal contradictions take place, which bring down the system. Nothing can remain stable as the social structure is dependent on the **economic base**. This is the basic premise of dialectical materialism.

Marx believed that the basic key to understanding the history of human society was exploitation. To Marx, class divisions were not simply between rich and poor. Classes were defined by how people stood in relation to the means of production. Those who produced food, clothing, shelter and so on have always been exploited. The surplus products they made were always controlled by a class of non-producers, except in very primitive societies. For example, in medieval, feudal societies everyone had to give a tenth of their produce (a tithe) to the Church.

To Marx, the history of the world was the history of class warfare. Classes must always be in competition with those that are above or below them. Because Marx believed in a dialectical structure to society, he saw it as a construction of opposites that would always be in conflict. He believed that classes only really existed because of their antagonism to each other, that they were defined by that antagonism and that people who lived in such a society could never live harmoniously together. He believed the course of history was economically determined and capitalism could only end in revolution.

Class in the capitalist society

In *The Communist Manifesto*, Marx described how capitalism had divided society into two opposing camps:

- Proletariat – *Workers who have no capital or means of production of their own. They are reduced to selling their labour power in order to live. 'The proletariat, is, in a word the working class of the nineteenth century.' (Engels, Principles of Communism)*
- Bourgeoisie – *The class of capitalists. Owners of the means of production and employers of wage labourers.*

Bourgeois is a term that is often used today in an insulting way to describe someone with narrow-minded middle-class tastes, but Marx based his structure of class on economic factors alone and not those of taste or habit. The use of the word in English probably came from the French Revolution, for the bourgeoisie were originally the French middle class, a class of merchants and small businessmen who became more powerful after the nobility fell out of favour with the masses.

Marx used the words bourgeoisie and capitalist interchangeably to describe the class that derived income from ownership or trade in capital assets, or from buying and selling commodities or services. He did make some differentiation between what he called 'functioning capitalists', those who manage industries, and 'mere coupon clippers', those who live off interest from shares or properties, but basically they all belonged to the one class. Their relation to the means of production was the same, for they owned them and used the labour of their workers to make a surplus product and extract profit.

On the other hand, the proletariat, or workers, did not own the means of production and had to sell their labour to the capitalists in order to live. There is no other way for workers to survive under a capitalist system, for they rely on wages to buy their means of subsistence: food, clothing and shelter.

Marx did acknowledge that other classes existed, but he believed they were becoming increasingly a part of the two main classes and these were becoming more and more polarized as capitalism progressed.

▶ *The self-employed or 'petty bourgeoisie' were usually those who had small family firms, owned some means of production and worked for themselves. Competition meant that they were increasingly being taken over by larger firms or put out of business entirely. The successful ones would rise to the ranks of the bourgeoisie, the rest would be pushed down into the proletariat.*
▶ *In Marx's day there was also a huge mass of domestic servants who had a better standard of living than many factory workers. However, they were dependent on their masters for their living and were basically still just selling labour power to the highest bidder. They would have more to lose in any class antagonism than factory workers for they were less independent.*
▶ *Managerial workers, such as factory supervisors, are also wage labourers but they are slightly more privileged than ordinary workers and again less likely to come into conflict with the capitalist than the workers because of their position.*

- ▶ Peasants worked largely on the land without much use of machinery up until the twentieth century and they still represented a large part of the European population in the time of Marx. He acknowledged that they were a separate class, but did not think they would be easy to involve in any class struggle. He wrote about this in The Eighteenth Brumaire of Napoleon Bonaparte, which examines the way that Napoleon III of France was supported by the peasants. Because they were isolated from each other, unlike the workers in factories, they would be difficult to organize but he believed that the urban proletariat could lead them into the class struggle.

- ▶ There was also what Marx called the 'stagnant element', the 'lumpenproletariat', the large mass of unemployables who do not really fit into society at all: 'thieves, vagabonds … the demoralised, the ragged'. Marx believed this class would get bigger as capitalism grew but he did not see them as being important in any class struggle because he felt they were too unreliable. Because they are not being exploited directly by the system as the workers are, they are less likely to come into conflict with the capitalist.

Marx recognized that these other classes did exist but he saw that under capitalism this class structure was becoming simpler and polarized into extremes. The bourgeoisie had created the need for the proletariat and now capitalism had expanded voraciously and was like a 'sorcerer who is no longer able to dominate the infernal powers he has conjured up'. In The Communist Manifesto he predicted that they had created the class that were going to be their gravediggers.

Marx saw that exploitation and oppression of the workers was the norm of the society he lived in; 'political power, properly so called, is merely the organised power of one class for oppressing another', he wrote in The Communist Manifesto.

The proletariat were being exploited, so why weren't they doing anything about it? Marx believed the answer lay in the alienation of the workers and in something he called **ideology**.

Ideology

According to Marx, each society is unique and has its own ideology: each society has its own assumptions about the nature of humanity and has its own morality and values. At the time that Marx was writing, most philosophers believed ideas and consciousness were the shaping forces of world history. Marx's materialist view divided society into the 'economic base' and the '**superstructure**'. He believed that the way people thought was a reflection of the economic base of the country that they lived in.

The economic base is really a combination of two things: '**productive forces**', as Marx called them, and '**relations of production**'.

Productive forces are material things used to produce commodities. These include things such as raw materials, machinery and the labour power of the workers who use them. For example, in a feudal society a weaver might use a hand-loom to turn sheep's wool into cloth, so the wool, loom and the work he does with them are productive forces.

Relations of production are the relationships between people or between people and things. For example, the loom may belong to a family of weavers who use it to make cloth that they can sell to rich customers. The relationships in the family, and of the family to their customers, are relations of production. In a feudal society, the relationship between a serf and his lord, described earlier in this chapter, is one example of a relation of production. Marx saw this economic base, formed by the productive forces and the relations of production, as intrinsic to the development of the superstructure of society.

The superstructure of society consists of its laws, culture, customs, religions and government. In a feudal society the economic base of society depended on its hierarchical structure. The loyalty of the serf to his lord was fundamental to the way society worked, so the superstructure of that society emphasized morality and religion, ideas of co-operation, obedience, and loyalty. This was entrenched in the morality of the Church and in the property laws. People 'belonged' to other people and to the land they worked on and they had a fixed place in the class hierarchy that was difficult to change; it was only in fairy stories that the goose girl got to marry the prince.

Marx believed that the economic base leads the development of the superstructure; the superstructure only exists in the form that it does because of the economic base. The productive forces changed radically during the Industrial Revolution. For example, small hand-looms were replaced by huge steam-driven ones in large factories, which needed hundreds of workers. It was no longer possible for society to function on a feudal basis; workers needed to be available on the free market and not tied to the land. The new relations of production were between boss and worker and so the political and legal superstructure had to change to accommodate the ideas of competitiveness and freedom of the individual.

Social consciousness, people's ideas, assumptions and ways of thinking reflected the society that they lived in, so society was shaped by the modes of production prevalent at that time. Marx believed the same economic base would sustain many different kinds of society, depending on historical and political factors. Even two fairly similar capitalist countries can have different social values. For example, although Britain, France and Germany are all capitalist countries in Europe they have very different cultures. Marx believed that the contradictions in the economic base were the driving force in historical struggle. He was not content to generalize on this point and spent a great many years of his life researching and analysing political and ideological data on class struggles in the histories of many countries.

Marx believed that the ideas that rule any country, and the laws that develop from them, must be the ideas of the ruling class. These rules naturally develop from the society as it changes. They are not worked out in advance. When feudalism developed into capitalism, nobody sat down and worked out that they would need to have a population that was free to move around the country to find work instead of being tied to the land. It was just that the new necessities of life meant that society had to develop in the way that it did. People had to take risks and work out solutions to the new problems that the new economic structure posed. Because the way that people actually think is influenced by the society around them and the society that went before, people find it difficult to develop entirely new ideas. They can only think in the way that their language and the concepts handed down to them allow. When people cannot see the way their beliefs are artificially constructed by society it is known in Marxist terms as false consciousness.

Insight

False consciousness is an important tenet of Marxist belief but it was a phrase that Marx did not use in any of his writings, although it was used by Engels.

Most people tend to believe that the world around them is in a finished, fixed form which cannot be changed. They do not examine the way in which the society around them came about or what processes it went through to get there. This makes it difficult for them to envisage any kind of change to the system. At the time Marx was writing, the divisions between the capitalist and the worker were seen as part of human nature and the natural order of society. This was reinforced by the fact that the capitalists control information, education, religion and entertainment. For example, in Victorian times most people would go to church. If we take a look at one of the popular hymns, *All Things Bright and Beautiful,* it contains the lines, 'the rich man in his castle, the poor man at his gate, God made them high or lowly and ordered their estate'. It was also a fact that most working-class people were not considered worthy of education and were not eligible to vote during most of the time Marx was alive. This must have affected the aspirations of people, as they would have valued themselves as not worthy citizens.

Marx believed that the only way to counteract this kind of thinking was a revolutionary workers' party, which would educate the workers so that they understood the ways in which they were being exploited and help them to revolt against it. Today we are much more aware of the conditioning of society and media manipulation, but only because Marx brought attention to the problem over a hundred years ago.

Class struggle

In the nineteenth century everybody took the class structure for granted, as if it had always existed in its current form. Marx believed that classes had never existed in exactly that way before because the economic structure of society had not existed in a capitalist form before. He believed that class structure had actually become much simpler than it had been before and it was the needs of the capitalist system that had actually brought the working class into existence. The capitalist system needed wage labourers to survive, but in creating this class it had actually sown the seeds of its own destruction.

The aim of the bourgeoisie, or capitalist class, was to increase their profits by any means possible. The aim of the proletariat, or workers, was to improve their living and working conditions. Marx believed these needs were obviously in conflict and would lead to class struggle and ultimately to revolution. Class struggle does not necessarily mean violent struggle, although Marx did believe that this would occur. Class struggle can be any social action that results from the different interests of classes; for example, demonstrating or writing a letter of protest.

In Marxist theory it is seen as necessary to allow class consciousness to develop. Marx talked of a class 'in itself' and a class 'for itself'.

▶ *A class 'in itself' refers to a group of individuals who share the same relationship to the means of production and share common interests.*
▶ *A class 'for itself' is a class that is conscious of these interests; a class that has discovered that it is alienated.*

The way for workers to realize they are alienated is through education and by political means. Marx believed that the very act of taking part in the class struggle would allow the working class to become aware and educated and would be of great benefit to them. 'In revolutionary activity the changing of oneself coincides with the changing of circumstances', he wrote in the *Theses on Feuerbach*.

Marx thought that the workers were in a unique position within the capitalist system as they were the only class capable of bringing about a revolution. They were the only class in society who could achieve a new form of society, a communist society.

Workers' power and education

Although the dialectical view of history states that capitalism will eventually bring about its own downfall, Marx did not think that it would happen automatically without anyone having to do anything. Although he was a great philosopher, he did not just talk idly of class struggle, he was also actively involved in the workers' movement, especially in his early life. Exiled in Paris he met with workers and was impressed by their character and strength; this led to his involvement with the League of the Just and the Communist League.

There were very few properly organized workers' groups in London when Marx moved there. Many of them had to be very secretive for fear of reprisals; anyone seen to be causing problems within the workplace was likely to be dismissed at the very least. But there were some movements towards change in society that had large elements of worker involvement.

THE CHARTISTS

Taking its name from the *Peoples' Charter* of 1838, this was a movement for political change in Britain. Although the Reform Act of 1832 had given many more people the vote in Britain, it was still true that most of them were middle-class property owners. Those who did not own property were not allowed to vote. From a modern-day perspective, this seems patently absurd and gives the lie to the idea that there is a long history of **democracy** in Britain. The Chartists were in favour of universal male suffrage: every man over 21 should be allowed a vote. Women were not even considered as voters, again this is something that seems absurd today, especially as many of the Chartists were women, including Engels' partner Mary Burns. The Chartists were a very diverse group, made up from many organizations and from many areas of society, but many were workers. At one rally it was estimated that 300,000 people attended and their weekly paper, the *Northern Star*, regularly sold 30,000 copies a week. Marx was very impressed by one of their leaders, Ernest Jones, and regularly wrote for his 'People's Paper'.

Although Chartism eventually petered out, the fact that there had been riots and demonstrations showed the feeling of the workers in the country and their desire to change the system. They could see that there was strength in numbers and value in being able to work together for a cause.

TRADE UNIONS

Trade unions developed out of trade guilds in the Middle Ages, but during the Industrial Revolution they began to grow in strength and to represent a wider range of the work force. They did not become legal in Britain until 1871, and so they were not a very powerful force before then as many workers were afraid to join. They were also rather elitist as they tended to represent craftsmen and not the unskilled. In continental Europe many trade union members were revolutionaries, but in Britain they were more moderate and worked alongside the Chartists in trying to get the vote.

Many modern-day Marxists are very disparaging about trade unions, believing they are part of the system, only negotiating for higher wages and not an instrument for change. Marx was not against unions, for he believed that a 'combination' of workers was the way forward; he hoped that if they became educated they would concentrate on changing the system, by demanding abolition of the wages system, and not just improving it.

The Communist League and class struggle

The Communist Manifesto was written by Marx and Engels in 1848 as a platform for the Communist League, a workingmen's association. The Communist League had developed out of the League of the Just; originally it consisted of only German members. At first it contained numerous anarchists whose idea was to destroy the factory system by violent means and return to an agricultural and small-craft society. Marx and Engels took on the task of re-organizing the Communist League; there were numerous disagreements with the anarchists, who eventually formed their own societies. Marx believed it was important for the ideas of the League to be spread around the world and eventually *The Communist Manifesto* was translated into many languages.

The Communist Manifesto was an appeal to the workers and it is one of Marx's most direct pieces of writing. The beginning describes the rise of the capitalist system and the class differences between the proletariat and the bourgeoisie. Marx then describes the future of the class struggle and its importance to the liberation of the worker.

He describes how dissatisfaction with working conditions and poor wages meant that workers clubbed together to form trade unions, to keep up the rates of wages and to plan revolts against capitalist domination. He notes that sometimes the revolts would turn into violent riots that, though successful locally, did not benefit the proletariat as a class. The benefit of these revolts was not in the result of the action taken but in the way in which the workers had grouped together to form unions.

Marx thought unions would keep expanding and this would be helped by modern forms of communication like the railways.

Insight

Marx was ahead of his time in understanding the importance of modern technology and communications to the revolutionary cause. Today the internet and mobile phones are vital tools for the organization of any anti-establishment group.

In Marx's time contact among groups could be made and eventually the numerous local struggles could be centralized to become a national struggle between the classes. Eventually, an international struggle would take place.

The proletariat needed to become better organized and stop any in-fighting between different factions. This would make them stronger and able to take advantage of divisions among the bourgeoisie. Eventually a revolution would occur, for only a revolution could overthrow a system that was spreading its tentacles all over the world.

The International Working Men's Association

Until the formation of the International Working Men's Association in 1864 there had been no real co-ordination between workers in the various capitalist economies that existed throughout the world. The First International, as it became known, was the first attempt to bring international workers together to fight a common cause. Any workers' groups that had previously existed tended to be secretive because of the risk of reprisals from the bourgeois capitalist class, so they attracted mostly radical conspirators. It was also true, as Marx pointed out, that the majority of the workforce accepted their exploitation as being natural. For this reason the majority of workers did not even belong to workers' associations in their own countries, let alone international ones.

Another barrier to international co-operation at this time was that there was little solidarity between citizens of the countries that made up Europe. For most of the Industrial Revolution, various countries within Europe had been at war with each other, or suffering civil war and revolution. Existing workers' associations focused on local issues. For example, in Germany they had become active under the leadership of Lassalle but confined their protests to their own country. In France the revolution had made the government grudgingly tolerant of the workers; fear of another revolution, driven by worker dissatisfaction, led to trade associations being allowed. These were under strict government supervision and regulated by the police in case they got out of hand. It was a meeting of these French trade associations and British trade unionists that forged the first link in the chain that led to the formation of the International.

The Great Exhibition of Modern Industry in 1863 was a showcase for British capitalist endeavour and drew in visitors from around the world. Among these were French labour leaders who came in an official delegation sent by the French emperor, Napoleon III. They met up with English labour leaders from the London Trades' Council to discuss tactics that could be used during strikes, the use of blackleg labour from abroad, wages, hours and pay. Following this meeting, they decided to form an association that would do more than just discuss the issues but would enable them to actively work together co-operatively on political and economic issues.

The first meeting took place in London in September 1864 and was chaired by Edward Beesly, a professor of Ancient History who was also a radical. Marx became involved because he was a well-known German émigré and activist. He was asked if he knew anyone to be a spokesman for the German workers and he recommended George Eccarius, a tailor whom he had assisted with the publication of articles on conditions in London tailoring shops. Marx attended the first meeting to support Eccarius but by the end of the evening he had been co-opted onto the committee.

It is often said by Marx's critics that he was not concerned with the reality of workers' lives and preferred to sit in his ivory tower writing, but his involvement with the International shows this is not the case. It is true he had a difficult and forceful personality and often fell out with his fellow members in the society, but he did work extremely hard to organize and support workers during his time at the International. This was in addition to his research and writing for *Das Kapital* and it brought him to the point of physical and mental exhaustion, even though it did not bring in any more money for his family.

Marx and Engels both became members of the International because it was a cause they believed in, but at the same time they realized that they were not workers themselves and hesitated to take office on the committee. However, when Marx saw the proposed constitution of the International, he decided to become more involved for he believed he could do a much better job!

He drew up the rules and principles and wrote the inaugural address which, after *The Communist Manifesto*, is one of the greatest appeals that he made to the workers. The constitution begins:

> *... the emancipation of the working classes must be conquered by the working classes themselves, that the struggle for the emancipation of the working classes means not a struggle for class privileges and monopolies, but for equal rights and duties, and the abolition of all class rule ...*

The inaugural address began with a survey of economic and social conditions since 1848, contrasting the lives of property owners with those of the workers. Marx likened capitalists to vampires who sucked the blood of children and sacrificed them in order to keep the economy going and described how working families starved in the midst of plenty. He wrote that although 1848 had been a year when revolution might have occurred throughout Europe, it had been thwarted, but that this meant the workers had since seen how they could work together as instruments of force. Since then, they had joined together to limit the length of the working day, but this was not enough. Co-operation would not be enough to stop the growth of the monopoly of capitalism and free the masses.

Marx finished with an appeal for the workers to realize that their vast numbers alone were not enough to make any difference, 'numbers weigh in the balance only if united by combination and led by knowledge'. The address ended with the powerful words that had concluded *The Communist Manifesto*, 'working men of all countries unite!'

The aims of the International were set out in the rules:

- ▶ *Establish close relations between workers in various countries and trades.*
- ▶ *Collect relevant statistics.*
- ▶ *Inform workers in one country of conditions, needs and plans of workers in another.*
- ▶ *Discuss questions of common interest.*
- ▶ *Co-ordinate simultaneous action in all countries in cases of international crisis.*
- ▶ *Publish frequent reports.*

The First International recruited many members and set up branches in Italy and Spain but it was eventually disbanded. One of the main problems was that workers from different countries wanted different things and came from different backgrounds. They did not even have a common aim, for although some of the members wanted revolution, some wanted to gain rights by peaceful means and they could not agree on how the campaign for workers' rights should be conducted. On the whole, the French were mainly Utopian Socialists and disliked trade unions, and the majority of the British contingent were trade unionists who were not interested in revolution. Even workers from the same country could not agree on aims and objectives; for example, many of the French were followers of Proudhon but many were revolutionaries. The eventual crisis that led to the downfall of the International was a result of personal animosity between Marx and Bakunin, but was really inevitable given that it was the first organization of its kind and that patriotism is such a strong issue for many people. Possibly, it is an example of the internal contradictions that Marx was so fond of writing about.

Is revolution inevitable?

Marx developed his views on revolution throughout his lifetime but on the whole he was in favour of revolution, although he did not believe it would necessarily have to be violent. At the conference of the International he addressed these words to the government, 'we will proceed against you by peaceful means where it is possible and with arms when it is necessary'.

The conclusion he drew from his dialectical study of society was that revolution was not only desirable but also inevitable because of the internal conflicts inherent in capitalism. According to Marx, these polar opposites could not exist together in a stable society; dialectical theory meant that the proletariat must overthrow the bourgeoisie.

'The history of all hitherto existing societies has been the history of class struggle', he said in *The Communist Manifesto*. He believed that a better society could then be built, a society based on the principles of communism. A communist society could not be built straight after a revolution, but would develop over time, after initial stages of socialism.

Marx was not the first to believe that society should be improved; many of his ideas were developed from those of the Utopian Socialists such as Owen and Fourier. They had criticized the capitalist system and shown how inhumane and oppressive it was. They believed in a socialist society where there was common ownership of the means of production. Where Marx differed from them was in the choice of method that would bring about this society. The Utopians believed reason was the best way to bring about a change in the views of society. They set up model communities and factories where hours were regulated; workers were treated fairly and given access to education, good homes and nourishing food. They believed these examples of **philanthropy** would be enough to bring about change in society.

Marx agreed with the humanitarian changes which were made, but thought that good housing, medical care, education and wage reforms did not get to the root of the problem, which was the exploitation of one class by another. If the economic base of society is the real source of the conflicts within it, no amount of workers' benefits will resolve the problem. The contradictions within the capitalist system will continue to accumulate. Change will only come about when workers take over factories, mines and banks by force: 'Material force must be overthrown by material force'.

Another reason Marx believed in the inevitability of revolution was his view of the state. He was the first to realize that 'the state' is not an impartial body that works for the benefit of everybody in society. Most materialist philosophers, including Hegel, viewed the state as a part of the natural order that was necessary to the working of society. Marx believed the state exists to protect the ruling class and suppress those that produce wealth for them. For example, in feudal societies laws were made in favour of the land-owning classes. Trespassing and poaching were often punished severely, even by death. In a capitalist society laws are passed which curb the power of trade unions and the media is controlled by the rich, who can use it to attack anyone who upsets the status quo. These factors make it even more likely that revolution must take place against the vested interests in capitalism. The state will try to block any peaceful or non-confrontational changes that undermine its powers of suppression.

In his early years, Marx believed that revolution would:

▸ *begin in the industrialized capitalist countries of Europe such as Britain and Prussia*
▸ *spread rapidly around the rest of the world because of the way in which countries had become economically dependent on each other.*

However, he did amend some of his ideas later in his life, which is why he was not totally wrong in predicting the future, for the first communist revolution was in Russia, a country based on a peasant economy. It remained the only communist country for nearly 30 years. Not long before his death, he saw that perhaps a revolution in Russia might occur in conjunction with one in Europe and could succeed because there was already a system of common ownership of land in place, and at the time of the Russian Revolution industrialization was beginning to expand rapidly.

Marx was disappointed in his lifetime as the predicted revolution did not occur, despite a number of simultaneous strikes and uprisings that happened throughout Europe in 1848. He and Engels became very excited by the bourgeois revolution in Germany that year and predicted it would soon spread, but when this did not materialize he wondered if perhaps the time was not quite right. In later years he predicted that workers might have to go through at least 50 years of struggle before they could change their circumstances, and that this would be a long-term process.

Marx was always against revolutionary terror of the kind that had happened in France and thought it showed immaturity on the part of the participants. For this reason, he was against revolution taking place too soon, when people were not educated enough to take part properly in the process of change.

As a philosopher, Marx saw benefits to the individual from revolution: 'In a revolution to change society men change themselves'. This is because he believed that people were not really free when they were subject to forces they couldn't understand. He hoped his writings would help them to realize these forces existed and that they were the products of the human mind. The human mind had created the economy and social structure that oppressed them, not a god or universal mind. When people realized this they would be free to take responsibility for their own actions and change both themselves and the world.

THINGS TO REMEMBER

▶ *Marx spent years refining his theories on the dialectical view of history and the development of the economy.*

▶ *He believed that society was always dominated by a ruling elite that controlled the means of production and the surplus products of the workers.*

▶ *He saw the history of society as a series of dialectical conflicts. Societies were continually destroyed by internal contradictions and then replaced.*

▶ *The capitalist system was the latest form of exploitation in a series of oppressive rules through history.*

▶ *The state was not an independent body but a tool that capitalists used to oppress the workers.*

▶ *Because the proletariat and bourgeoisie could not exist together in a stable society, revolution would be inevitable.*

7

Further Marxist thought

In this chapter you will learn:
- *what Marx believed might happen after the revolution*
- *about the dictatorship of the proletariat*
- *how Marx and Engels thought a communist society might work*
- *Marx's views on religion, women's rights and the family, art and culture, freedom and the individual.*

Although Marx wrote a great deal about the way in which the relationship between society and the economy had developed throughout history, he did not write much about how these would develop after the revolution that he had predicted. He believed a classless communist society would be the result of the revolution, but he did not really define how this society might be run. This is hardly surprising as his view of the world was a materialist one; anything that might happen in the future was a supposition and could not be examined. As he believed that the structure of society was based on the economic factors existing at the time, he did not think it possible to predict in advance any details of what that structure would be like. He made a few predictions about what might happen and some of these were influenced by the ideas of the Utopian Socialists and the French communists, although he did not agree with a lot of their more Romantic ideals.

He did not write in detail about the structure of any future communist society, but he thought deeply about the relationships between people within that society. In his writing he looked at the world in a new way and shed new light on the relationships between individuals and the society they lived in. His ideas were considered extremely radical in their day but today we take many of them for granted in Western society; for example, equal rights for men, women and children.

After the revolution

Marx did not write a great deal about the form that society would take after the revolution, or how it would be organized. He believed that society would have to become communist in the long term, but there would have to be a transitional phase before this could occur. At first, society would be 'stamped with the birthmarks' of the past capitalist society it had emerged from, like a child from the womb. Marx did not believe that it would be possible to go directly from a capitalist society to a communist one, there would have to be an intermediate stage between the two known as socialism. Socialism in the Marxist sense is just a descriptive word for the intermediate stage between capitalism and communism. Today the word socialism has become a much less easily defined term, referring to any system where there is state control, planning and ownership of the means of production. There is also some element of social care for the sick, children, the elderly and those in extreme poverty. (Many would argue that those countries that declare themselves to be communist states are actually only at the state of socialism.)

Insight
It is important that when you read anything on socialism that you understand how the author defines the term in the text.

Under socialism there would be a dictatorship of the proletariat. Marx wrote about this in "The Class Struggles in France" written for the *Neue Rheinische Zeitung Revue* in 1850. Here he wrote that, 'the class dictatorship of the proletariat would be a necessary stage for the "abolition of class distinctions generally"'. He also wrote in the *Critique of the Gotha Programme*, 'Between capitalist and the communist society there lies the period of the revolutionary transformation of the one into the other. Corresponding to this is also a political transition period in which the state can be nothing but the revolutionary dictatorship of the proletariat.'

Insight

The *Critique of the Gotha Programme* was a commentary made about the Gotha Conference and was not published until after Marx's death. It is one of the few texts where Marx discusses the ways in which a future communist society might be organized.

Dictatorship of the proletariat was a phrase that Marx hardly used at all in his work but the theory was developed by Lenin, the Russian communist leader, at the start of the first Communist Revolution, and came to popular attention. Dictatorship of the proletariat is a phrase that people today tend to relate to the way both Lenin and **Stalin** ruled the Soviet Union using non-democratic methods. Marx used the word dictatorship in its original sense: rule by a group of people, rather than by one despot. It was based on the model of the Roman dictatura: rule by an elite in times of crisis.

Marx believed that capitalist society was in effect a 'dictatorship of the bourgeoisie', for they controlled society through laws, education and ideology and would not give this up easily. He believed that the only way that the workers would be able to keep hold of power after a revolution was for them to take control of the state apparatus themselves and to rule in their own interests. He had studied the Paris commune and was impressed by the way in which it was proposed that all officials, including judges, were to be voted for by universal suffrage. All officials were to be paid the same as workers and the standing army was to be replaced by a citizens' army. The police and clergy would not be allowed to hold political office. In this way, the workers would have control of the apparatus of society – schools, courts, prisons, the armed forces – but in an open and democratic way. It would also prevent the bourgeoisie from being able to reorganize a counter-revolution easily.

In 1917 Lenin developed the idea of the dictatorship of the proletariat in *The State and Revolution*. His definition of dictatorship as 'exercise of power without law', was very different from that used by Marx. Lenin believed that because ideology and false consciousness had such a hold over the minds of everyone, certain select members of the Communist Party would have to act as the **vanguard of the proletariat**. They would lead society into a true understanding of communism. He believed that, even after a revolution, the bourgeoisie would remain stronger than the proletariat because they would still have money and property, better education and connections, and be more experienced in public office and in the 'art of war'. He proposed that a 'class dictatorship' was necessary in Russia and force should be used against the former ruling class.

During the Russian Civil War, all political parties, except the Bolshevik ones that supported Lenin, were abolished one by one on various trumped-up charges, so that eventually only one party remained: the **Bolsheviks**. After Lenin's death, in-fighting among the Bolsheviks was eventually overcome by the iron rule of Stalin.

Insight

The Bolsheviks were members of the Marxist Russian Social Democratic Labour Party which split away from the more moderate Mensheviks in 1903. They eventually became the ruling communist party in the Soviet Union.

Freedom of speech was virtually abolished and any dissent was ruthlessly suppressed. One ruling elite was replaced by another; this was a distortion of what Marx had believed in.

Communist society

Marx believed that once the proletariat had achieved state power they could take control of the means of production and, eventually, class distinctions would be abolished and a classless communist society would be the result. Society would not be based on one class exploiting another class; workers would be in control of the means of production and they would use the wealth produced for the good of society as a whole. Society would be a self-governing community.

Marx believed society would eventually be stateless because he believed the state was a tool that let one branch of society oppress another. He felt that when classes were finally abolished then 'the power of the state, whose function is to keep the great majority of producers beneath the yoke of a small minority of exploiters, will disappear and government functions will be transformed into simple administrative functions'.

After the revolution, the state would 'wither away' as there would be no oppression, but it would take time. Engels said that 'the proletariat seizes political power and turns the means of production in the first instance into state property. But in doing this it abolishes itself as the proletariat'. In order to do this, society would need to be more productive with a much shorter working day so that people would have time to participate in running society.

Because he believed the ownership of property defines the class system, it was important to Marx that private property should be abolished. This would mean that classes would eventually cease to exist, so there would be no inequality and no need for further class struggle. He also thought that when the means of production were centralized, private property would disappear and money would then cease to exist.

Marx and Engels firmly believed that the revolution would be an international one. This would mean that the army would have a purely internal peacekeeping function and money would not need to be spent on defence.

The main writings we have on the form that a communist society would take are *The Principles of Communism*, written by Engels in 1847. These set out the views of the Communist League, of which Marx was a member. These are the main points of the document:

- *Limitation of private property through progressive taxation, inheritance tax and abolition of inheritance rights for the family.*
- *Capitalists to be expropriated through competition with state industry and partial compensation.*
- *Confiscation of the possessions of emigrants and rebels against the majority.*
- *Central organization of wages for workers on the land or in factories. Competition between workers to be abolished.*
- *All members of society to be equally liable for work until private property is abolished. Industrial armies to be formed, especially for agriculture.*
- *Private banks to be suppressed and money and credit to be centralized in national banks.*
- *State-owned factories, workshops, etc. to be developed as far as economically feasible; agriculture to be improved.*
- *Education for all children at state schools, paid for by the State.*
- *Communal dwellings to be built on waste land to combine the best of rural and urban life.*
- *Unhygienic, badly built slum housing to be destroyed.*
- *Equal inheritance rights for children born out of wedlock.*
- *Transport to be **nationalized**.*

It was not considered feasible that all these changes could take place at once. It was felt that once one change was made others would follow and they would accumulate. The abolition of private property would be the first step and then agriculture, transport and trade would be centralized.

Marx and Engels didn't consider the future communist society to be a utopian one or that it was based on utopian principles. They wrote in *The Communist Manifesto*, 'the theoretical conclusions of the communists are in no way based on the ideas or principles that have been invented, or discovered by this or that would-be universal reformer'. Engels was a great admirer of Fourier though, as can be seen in his idea of building communal dwellings combining urban and rural living.

Marx did not want a return to some idealized rural society; he saw that technological progress was one of the main benefits that capitalism had brought to society and he believed that development of this would lead to huge improvements in society. In this way, his ideas were closer to those of Saint-Simon's technocracy. In the *Grundrisse*, Marx writes that work would become 'an automatic system of machinery'. He believed that manual labour would be reduced by a mixture of 'social combination' and the 'technological application of the natural sciences'. This would allow for more leisure time and time for education. It would help society to become stateless because the working week would be shorter and everyone would be able to participate in running society. It would also lead to material abundance for all.

Surplus labour would still exist but it would not be hidden by any kind of exploitation or fetishism. In the third volume of *Das Kapital*, Marx had the idea that these surpluses would be used in a kind of welfare state. Everyone who could work would have to work, but the surplus product would be set aside and divided between those who could not support themselves; those who 'on account of age are not yet, or no longer able to take part in production'. He did not believe that anyone else should be supported by the state though, for he also wrote that, 'all labour to support those who do not work would cease'.

Communist society would be a hardworking and productive place, but both Marx and Engels hoped that work in a communist society would be enjoyable and not an oppressive means of survival. It was hoped that after the initial stages of communism, where people were still attached to old capitalist ways of thinking, then a communist society would take into account people's varying needs and abilities. Marx wrote in the *Gotha Programme*:

> *In a higher phase of communist society, after the enslaving subordination of the individual to the division of labour, and therewith also the antithesis between mental and physical labour, has vanished; after labour has become not only a means of life but life's prime want; after the productive forces have also increased with all-round development of the individual, and all the springs of co-operative wealth flow more abundantly – only then can the narrow horizon of bourgeois right be crossed in its entirety and society inscribe on its banners: From each according to his ability, to each according to his needs!*

Religion

'Religion is the opium of the people', is one of Marx's most famous quotations. Opium is an addictive drug that dulls the senses; Marx believed that religion had a similar function in capitalist society.

Marx had seen some of the problems that religion caused to his own family when his father renounced his Jewish faith. Prussia was an anti-Semitic country and Jews were not allowed to hold public office. He saw that religion was a part of the state system that could be used as a form of oppression and as a part of the false consciousness that added to the alienation of the populace.

Marx himself was an atheist and was greatly influenced by materialist philosophers and free thinkers such as Hume and Diderot, who had concentrated on finding rational arguments against religion. Being believers in scientific order and rationalism, they thought they could prove by scientific means that God could not exist. They thought that most people had a superstitious belief in God that would disappear when they were enlightened by the powers of reason.

Marx agreed with these rationalist philosophers to some extent, but his views on alienation meant that he believed that a purely rationalist view of the world was not enough to change it. He was greatly influenced by Feuerbach, who said the essence of Christianity was the essence of mankind itself. Marx believed that God was created by human consciousness and was a product of human minds, but he wanted to understand why people worshipped God and why their religious beliefs took the form that they did. Again, he spent many years researching and analysing societies past and present, this time to find evidence on the question of religion.

Eventually, he came to the conclusion that religion is part of the ideological make-up of society:

▶ *In primitive societies, where people's lives are dependent on their relationship with the natural world, religion helps to unite them with nature. Natural forces are worshipped as gods and the natural cycles of their world become part of the religion.*
▶ *In more developed societies, people become freed from their dependence on nature by use of technology but they feel alienated from the society because they have little control over their daily lives. People then use religion as a means of expressing their frustrations.*

Marx believed that any fulfilment people achieved from religion was illusory because religion is just another form of alienation. People do not realize they are not free and, until they do, they cannot change society so there is little to be achieved by demonstrating a lack of science and reason in religion. In this way, he differed from the philosophers who came before him; Hegel, Feuerbach and the other Young Hegelians. They believed the alienation people felt was because they did not understand the progress of the universal mind and once they saw their place in this, through philosophical enlightenment, they would see things clearly, as they truly are, and without any religious false consciousness. Their lives would then have meaning.

Marx believed that people felt that their lives were meaningless because they were actually meaningless. Capitalism is a social system that means we are unfulfilled as human beings. 'Religious distress is at the same time the expression of real distress and also the protest against real distress. Religion is the sigh of the oppressed creature, the heart of a heartless world, just as it is the spirit of spiritless conditions. It is the opium of the people.'

Marx could see that religion served a very important function in capitalist society. Religion acknowledges the alienation of the individual but says this is because they are separated from God. This is useful, for it stops people questioning whether their feelings are due to the way their society is structured. They feel that alienation is a part of the natural condition of humanity.

Religion leads people to believe that there is a purpose to their suffering which they might not understand but gives promises of an afterlife if they follow certain spiritual practices. It exaggerates the alienation of the individual and offers them a long-term cure at the same time. It also brings reassurance, for many people need their religious illusions as a prop and as a comfort in a harsh environment.

Marx saw that merely understanding the problem was not enough; philosophy itself cannot change the world. Understanding why you feel alienated is only the beginning.

Religion will only cease to exist when alienation ceases to exist and this cannot happen until certain classes are no longer oppressed and everybody becomes equal in a communist society: 'The abolition of religion, as the illusory happiness of men, is a demand for their real happiness. The call to abandon their illusions about their condition is a call to abandon a condition which requires illusions.'

Women's rights and the family

In *The Communist Manifesto*, Marx and Engels take great pains
to point out that the communists are not about to introduce
'a community of women' and break up the family. They had been
accused of this in the press several times that year. Some of their
liberal views on the institution of marriage shocked staid Victorian
Britain and caused a minor sensation. At that time, women in
most capitalist countries did not have the vote and in the eyes of
the law they were seen as possessions belonging to their husbands.
A community of women implied women who would be free to give
their sexual favours to anyone they chose. Marx pointed out in
The Communist Manifesto that the bourgeoisie used their wives
like instruments of production and feared that, as instruments of
production were to be exploited, then the same fate would happen
to their wives. He argued that marriage could be considered as
a legalized form of prostitution, 'Bourgeois marriage is in reality
a system of wives in common and thus at the most what the
communists might possibly be reproached with is that they want to
introduce, in substitution for a hypocritically concealed, an openly
legalized community of women.' He draws the conclusion that only
through the abolition of the class system would prostitution, 'both
public and private', be abolished.

Much of Marxist thought on women and the family arises from
the work of Engels. There are no other communist writers of that
time who wrote on the rights of women as being separate from the
rights of workers as a whole class.

Insight

Engels was probably influenced on these points by his
Chartist lover, Mary Burns.

Engels was a great admirer of Fourier, an early advocate of
women's rights who invented the term feminism and proposed
a utopia of communes and 'free love'. In 1845 Engels wrote
The Origin of the Family, Private Property and the State. In this,

he argues that monogamous marriage is a social institution that exists in relation to private property and that women must be economically independent from men before they can be truly emancipated. One of the most well-known quotations from this work is, 'The modern individual family is based on the open or disguised enslavement of the woman.' Engels believed that all women were a slave class under capitalism, proletariat and bourgeois alike:

> *When she fulfils her duties in the private service of her family, she remains excluded from public production and cannot earn anything; and when she wishes to take part in public industry and earn her living independently, she is not in a position to fulfil her family duties. What applies to the woman in the factory applies to her in all professions, right up to medicine and law.*

Marx wanted everybody to be equal – men, women and children – and he believed that a communist society without private property would ensure this. He felt that relations between the sexes and relations between parents and children were corrupted by wage labour and private property. In *The Communist Manifesto* he wrote, 'All family ties between the proletariat are torn asunder, children transformed into simple articles of commerce and instruments of labour.'

Class divisions at that time meant that men, women and children from the working class laboured for long hours in factories and mines. They had few opportunities for health care or education. Women in the middle classes did not work outside the home after marriage and it was not always seen as necessary to educate girls. Marx believed that marriage could never be an equal partnership when women were treated as second-class citizens and men were seen as the head of the household, for this stopped women from reaching their true potential as individuals.

In an ideal communist society, Marx believed there would be equal access for all to work and education. Adequate childcare facilities would mean that women would no longer have to be financially dependent on their husbands. Women would not be financially disadvantaged by bearing children and caring for them. Marx believed that bringing all women into the workplace was the first step in giving them equality. It would be the first step in getting them involved in planning the economy, and so changing society. It would also be the first step in abolishing prostitution, which he saw as a by-product of the capitalist system that viewed everything in financial terms.

Marx always thought that it was not enough just to pass liberal laws giving rights to minorities if the whole structure of society and the economy remains the same. Laws can be passed to give rights to women, but it is only when the ideology of the society changes, so that women do not bear the entire burden of care of the young and elderly, that women will be emancipated. This proved to be correct in many so-called communist societies where women did a day's work, often in physically demanding jobs, but found that it was still their job to do the housework and the shopping. Modern capitalist society is quite often the same.

Feminism grew rapidly in the twentieth century from small beginnings in the nineteenth century, and although many modern-day feminists would disagree with the views of Marx and Engels and their analysis of the place of women, it cannot be denied that they were some of the earliest social reformers to look at the position of women in society in a systematic way. Marxist feminism is still an important part of the whole feminist movement and the emphasis of Marxist feminists is mainly on the belief that capitalism is the root of women's oppression and that women's subordination is really a form of class oppression. A lot of their work is centred around the workplace; examining why women still have low wages and the ways in which women's domestic work is trivialized by capitalism. Many of them admire the way Marx exposed how social, economic and political structures can cause alienation.

Art and culture

Marx believed art and culture were important parts of any society. He believed an appreciation of these is vital for everybody in a society, for they help us to understand our society as well as ourselves. He was very fond of using quotations from Greek literature and Shakespeare in his work; *Das Kapital* is full of such references. This made it difficult for ordinary working people to understand; most preferred to read Engels, who wrote in a more straightforward manner. Of course many workers at that time could not read at all because they were not educated. This illustrates Marx's first point:

▶ *Art is mainly for the minority. In a capitalist system, it is selected by a minority. Their freedom to enjoy art is at the expense of those who work to produce the wealth that gives them the money and leisure time to enjoy art. Artists have to supply art that will satisfy the requirements and taste of this minority. This leads to his second point.*

▶ *Capitalist society tends to see everything in financial terms. Everything is given a financial 'value'. Freedom of expression, craftsmanship and making things for their own sake become subordinated by time and money.*

Marx believed that art, like society, developed as a series of dialectical contradictions.

As members of a society, artists, writers and musicians must also be influenced by the prevailing ideology. There will always be a few who struggle to express themselves in new ways, contradicting the old forms of artistic expression. In this way, art can subvert the bourgeois prejudices that prevail in a capitalist society.

Marx's view was that, in the ideal communist society, everyone will have access to the cultural heritage of society and artistic activities will stop being the preserve of a privileged minority.

Freedom and the individual

Marx saw individuals as products of the society to which they belong. Each society has its own view on individuality because each society has its own ideology. Every different social system will place a different emphasis on the relationship between the individual and the society. In certain societies, for example capitalism, the rights of the individual are highly prized. In other societies the rights of the group are seen as more important than the rights of the individual.

Marx wrote of the alienation in the capitalist system, which led to competitive struggle between individuals. He felt this was a necessary stage on the way to communism, where people would find their true individuality without the need for destructive competitiveness. Because Marx believed it was the capitalist work system that stopped the individual reaching his true potential, he felt only the rise of the proletariat and the change to a communist society would allow the individual his full rights. In the proposed communist society:

▶ *Labour would be planned for producing the means of life, according to agreed needs.*
▶ *Labour time would be reduced to increase free time for everyone. This would lead to artistic and scientific development for all and would lead to greater self-knowledge.*

Marx did not think that greed and envy were intrinsic to human nature, and stated that if private property and capitalist ways of working were changed to a system of communal property and a communal means of production, then people would no longer be in competition with each other. There would be no false consciousness and no exploitation. He wrote in the *Gotha Programme* that communism would mean an end to the 'enslaving subordination of the individual to the division of labour'. He believed that capitalism forced people into demeaning work and kept them from improving their status. He hoped that:

> *In a communist society, where nobody has one exclusive sphere of activity but each can become accomplished in any branch he wishes, society regulates the general production and thus makes it possible for me to do one thing today and another tomorrow, to hunt in the morning, fish in the afternoon, rear cattle in the evening, criticise after dinner, just as I have a mind, without ever becoming hunter, fisherman, shepherd or critic.*

At the time Marx was writing, workers' groups were fighting for the essential rights of freedom:

- ▶ *freedom of speech*
- ▶ *freedom of assembly*
- ▶ *freedom of the press*
- ▶ *equality under the law*
- ▶ *equal rights to vote.*

Marx did not disagree with any of these rights, but he believed that as long as the economic base of society was still capitalist then people were not free, even if they had the rights by law. For example, although in the eyes of the law everybody is equal, those who are better off can afford better representation in court; there may be freedom of the press but only the very rich can afford to own a major newspaper. It is only when capitalism is overthrown by revolution that true freedom will occur.

THINGS TO REMEMBER

▶ *Society after the revolution would eventually be communist, after the initial stage of socialism. The means of production would be centralized, private property would be abolished and money would cease to exist.*

▶ *Before a communist state existed, an intermediate socialist state would exist under the dictatorship of the proletariat.*

▶ *Religion is the opium of the people. It helps people to overcome their feelings of alienation and to express their frustrations, but the support it gives is illusory.*

▶ *Everyone in society should have equal rights. Women should not be excluded from the workplace because they care for children and the elderly.*

▶ *Art and culture are important because they allow people to understand the society they live in but under capitalism they are a minority interest for the elite.*

▶ *Art can be used to subvert the ideology of a society.*

▶ *Individuality is a concept that changes with the ideology of a society.*

▶ *In a capitalist system, individuality is important but alienation means that people are not free.*

▶ *All the above injustices could only be remedied in a communist system.*

▶ *People may be given rights under a capitalist system but, until the structure of society is changed, the advantages they gain are not true rights.*

8

Marxism after Marx – ideas that changed the world

In this chapter you will learn:
- *about the spread of Marxist thought*
- *how socialism developed away from communism*
- *what led to revolution in Russia and China*
- *about the Cold War*
- *about the decline of communism*

Marxism is a term that can be used in a number of different ways. It is used to describe political systems where the ideas of Marx are allegedly put into practice. It is also used to describe social, philosophical and political theories based on the ideas of Marx. Marx died over a century ago and his ideas have been discussed and have evolved in many different forms since then. Many branches of Marxist thought have developed throughout the world and schools of Marxism have flourished in academic circles. In this chapter, I will be looking at the way that Marx's ideas spread around the world and influenced political systems. The development of communism as a political system, beginning with the Russian Revolution of 1918, led to Marx's ideas becoming a major driving force in the history of the twentieth century. They were also a major part of the early socialist movement, which developed out of the labour movement.

In addition to his few books, Marx wrote numerous articles, pamphlets and speeches, many of which were not published until after his death. Because of the vast body of his work and its complexity, it is easy for people to interpret his ideas in their own way and claim that their interpretation is the 'true' meaning of Marxism. In some ways it is similar to interpretation of the Bible; there are many kinds of churches that call themselves Christian but they all have their own ways of worshipping God and many believe that their way is the 'right' way. Many different regimes call themselves Marxist or communist, but they do not necessarily have similar ideologies or political systems.

In fact, they may well have very little in common with the original ideas of Marx, except for the use of his name. Marx became so upset by the many misinterpretations of his ideas that it is reported that he said, 'All I know is that I am not a Marxist'. Many countries declared themselves as communist, Marxist or socialist during the twentieth century: some after one revolution, some after successive coups and revolutions and some after no revolution at all. Each one of these countries could have several books written about them. It is not possible in a short chapter to go into detail about every communist state in the world and its relationship to the works of Marx. The intention is to look at some of the ways that his ideas were interpreted and disseminated after his death and how they led to a change in the political structure of the world.

The spread of Marxist thought

Karl Marx died in 1883 but his work carried on. Shortly before his death, Marx had been worried about what would happen to the volumes of *Das Kapital* he had started writing and had remarked that perhaps Engels would be able to 'do something' with his papers. Engels considered himself to be a 'mere talent' compared to the genius of Marx; he wrote to an old friend, F. A. Sorge, after Marx's death, 'the proletarian movement will go on, but the centre is gone'. Engels then had to become that centre. Marx had died without making a will, but the bulk of his correspondence and notes were passed on to Engels and he decided to devote most of the rest of his life into sorting them out and making them fit for publication. He shared some of the work with Marx's youngest daughter Eleanor (Tussy). They were among the few people who could read Marx's terrible handwriting and understand the symbols he invented in his notes. Although Engels edited and published the later volumes of *Das Kapital*, it was Eleanor who did a lot of the background work: researching, checking and annotating references. She also did a lot of translation work. Volume 2 of *Das Kapital* was first published in Germany in 1885 and Volume 3 was published in 1894. Although the first English translation sold badly, the second edition, brought out in 1895, sold out in a few months; the philosophy of communism that Marx and Engels had developed together began to spread around the world, mainly through the labour movement and working men's groups.

Engels became a popular figure among the new Marxist groups that began springing up as a result of the translations of Marx's works; he gave advice to labour movements and to those who were beginning to organize the new International Working Man's Association. He wrote articles in German, Austrian and French publications and became involved with working men's associations throughout Europe, including Spain, Denmark, Bulgaria and Serbia. As he knew Russian, he became a link between German and Russian Marxists. In 1889 he met Plekhanov, a Russian communist leader, who travelled to London especially to see him, and he began to write for the first Russian Marxist periodical.

When the Second International was formed, Engels didn't take part in it directly but he was influential behind the scenes as an advisor and translator. The international labour movement was growing rapidly, and it was through this that the ideas of Marx began to take hold on the minds of workers throughout the world. Marx's ideas became the basis of many socialist parties throughout Europe, although many of them did not advocate revolution, preferring to change society by means of reform. Marx's analysis of the capitalist system and the way in which it exploited workers gave them a base on which to structure their justification for reform. From the widely differing versions of communism that developed after Marx's death there emerged two main strands:

▶ **Evolutionary communism** – *Evolutionary communists believe in the power of the evolution of society. Communism will come about through the natural progress of society and the disintegration of the capitalist system, due to its internal flaws. Evolutionary communists resemble Social Utopians to some extent in their belief that society can be changed for the better without revolution. These 'reformists' want to work within existing political systems.*

▶ **Revolutionary communism** – *Revolutionary communists believe the power of revolution is the only way to change society. Communism will come about only through the overthrow of the bourgeoisie by violent means, including* **terrorism**. *Terrorists do not necessarily believe the state can be defeated by their actions but hope to destroy the morale of the people and their support for the government.*

As Engels travelled though Europe speaking to workers' groups, the crowds coming to listen became larger and larger and he began to get standing ovations. In the fourth German edition of *The Communist Manifesto*, he expressed a deep regret that Marx could not see how much the international labour movement was growing. At the age of 75, Engels began writing the history of the First International when he became ill. He died in August 1895 of cancer of the oesophagus; he was cremated and his ashes were scattered off Beachy Head on the south coast of England.

It was then that Eleanor Marx and her partner Edward Aveling took possession of all Marx's papers and sorted and stored them. They were well-known figures in socialist circles in London and had both been members of the Democratic Federation, led by Henry Hyndman, in the 1880s. They then became part of the Socialist League, led by William Morris.

Eleanor Marx was a popular speaker on socialist topics and on
women's rights. She led mass rallies on the shorter working day in
Hyde Park and played an active part in organizing strikes among
women who worked in match factories. She wrote about her
father and his work, fundraised in the USA for the German Social
Democratic Party and in 1889 she was a delegate for the Second
International in Paris. Sadly, her work in disseminating her father's
ideas was cut short as she committed suicide in 1898; it was thought
this was due to problems in her relationship with Edward Aveling.

The development of socialism

The socialist and communist movements in Europe at the end
of the nineteenth century were closely intertwined. At first, they
both mainly concentrated on workers' rights and on universal
suffrage. Both movements were based on the theories of Marx, but
it became apparent as time went on that some people were more
moderate than others and a split began between the followers of
evolutionary and revolutionary strands of thought. This eventually
led to the break up of the Second International. Those with a more
revolutionary and communist interpretation of Marx broke away
to form the Third International during the First World War, while
the reformists developed social democracy or socialism. Socialism
is a word that can be confusing in Marxist literature because the
term in general use differs from the Marxist term. Generally it is
taken to indicate belief in a socio-economic system with some kind
of state or collective ownership of the means of production, but it
is a very vague term that covers many diverse types of government.
In the main, it differs from communism because this is usually

identified with a one-party totalitarian state. In classical Marxism, Marx is often described as a 'scientific socialist' and socialism refers to the period occurring just after the revolution before true communism is reached. This is how confusion often occurs.

The socialist movement developed from the communist one, so the ideas of Marx were an important part of doctrine at the beginning of the twentieth century. The First International was the first place where socialist doctrine was promoted on an international scale and Marx's involvement with this led to his ideas being accepted by workers around the world, but especially in Europe. As more and more countries brought in universal suffrage, more working men began to rise to positions of power within government and could start to put socialist ideas into practice. This led to the development of a lot of socialist ideas, such as the welfare state and nationalization of industries, without the need for revolution. As conditions for working people improved, most of them felt there was no need to have a revolution at all. For example, in Britain work by the intellectuals of the Fabian Society finally led to the Labour Party being formed in 1906 and a similar party was formed in France in 1905.

Insight

The Fabian Society began in 1884 and still exists today. It is an intellectual socialist movement that works towards gradual change in society rather than revolution.

In Germany Karl Kautsky led the Social Democratic Workers' Party, and although this was ostensibly Marxist and revolutionary, it eventually became reformist. The more radical members split off to follow Rosa Luxumberg, a Polish-born Marxist who was eventually beaten to death by state police during a failed communist uprising in Berlin in 1919. The period after the First World War was probably the time when the international communist revolution was most likely to have happened, for there were uprisings in Germany, Hungary and Finland and a lot of communist activity in other European states. However, brutally repressive regimes crushed the Communist opposition and some historians consider this as the beginning of the rise of **fascism**.

The First World War put an end to much of the internationalist nature of the socialists, as most of the reformists had strong patriotic tendencies and they supported their own countries rather than a worldwide revolution. Lenin decreed that the war was an imperialist conflict and called for all true communists to forge a worldwide revolution, but he had to fight to bring about communism in Russia without much support.

Russian communism

Russia was the first communist country in the world. The type of communism that eventually evolved there had little in common with Marx's thoughts on how communism should develop after the revolution. However, because it was the first communist country, and the only communist country for many years, people often believe that Russian communism is 'true communism'.

The first revolutionary communists were the Bolsheviks in Russia, led by Lenin. They overthrew the Romanov dynasty that had ruled the country in a feudal manner for 300 years. The communist uprising of 1917 came as a surprise to most of the world, which had never heard of communism or Karl Marx.

Marx predicted that revolution would be started by the industrial working class or proletariat. This class hardly existed at all in Russia in 1917. It seems curious that the first communist revolution took place in a country that had a large peasant population – at least 80 per cent of the population as a whole. In his later years, Marx had not entirely ruled out the idea that a Russian revolution might occur without the country first passing through a period of capitalist society because of its unique social structure.

The Russian Empire at that time was vast, and compared with much of Europe it was very backward and had little industrialization. Three quarters of the people lived off the land and barely subsisted through the harsh winters. Although feudalism had been officially abolished in 1861, the serfs had to pay compensation to their landlords and were worse off than before.

At the time of the revolution Russia was ruled by the autocratic leader Tsar Nicholas the Second. He nominated friends and family to the State Council, which was the chief governing body. It was obvious to outsiders that the state was corrupt but it was not obvious that a revolution would take place. Although country landlords had been made poor, they were passive and the peasants were loyal to the tsar. The urban working class were a very small part of the population and were badly organized. Although the government was inefficient, it was ruthless in repressing any signs of anti-government activity. The press was censored and dissidents were sent to live as outcasts in the harsh terrain of Siberia; traditions that the communists followed when they came into power.

Marxism came to Russia through the work of Georgi Plekhanov, son of a landowner who moved to Europe. He was the first native Russian to write about Marxism as it applied to his home country. His ideas were carried by students to factories and towns and one of his chief converts was Vladimir Illyich Ulyanov, later to be known as Lenin. Lenin was sent to Siberia for three years for preaching the words of Marx to factory workers. He became a ruthless leader of the people and took advantage of the chaos in his country to take power. Although Lenin was a charismatic leader, it was not just his interpretation of Marx that led to revolution. It was a war that Marx could not have foreseen that became the catalyst for revolution and led to the first communist state.

Russia was already ravaged by industrial unrest and social dissatisfaction when the First World War began. Initial patriotism turned into discontent, especially as many lives and areas of land were lost. Refugees caused a housing crisis, people were starving and prices were rising. The population became demoralized and war-weary. Lenin realized that peace was important to the population and insisted that the war would only end if capitalism was overthrown. He called for the peasants to redistribute the land and for political power to be held by the soviets, a kind of local council. The Bolsheviks took power in October 1917 and declared a decree on peace. Lenin inaugurated the dictatorship of the proletariat to justify the role of the Communist Party, which did not have the complete support of the population. He believed it was important to create a true 'socialist man' who was free from the false consciousness that alienated him. The Bolsheviks then changed the name of their revolutionary party to The Communist Party and eventually the Third International became Comintern. It was transformed from an independent international organization of communist countries into an agency of the Soviet Union which co-ordinated world communism.

The communists hoped that spontaneous revolutions would take place throughout Europe following the example of Russia, but they never took place. Marx had seen this as imperative for the Russian state if it was to develop into a communist society after revolution, but Russia was the only socialist state in Europe for some time. After many years of civil war in Russia, a so-called communist state eventually evolved which had very little to do with the society envisaged by Marx and Engels. At first, things looked favourable: free enterprise was abolished; land, banks, foreign trade and shipping were **nationalized**. These measures should have been the start of the ideal communist state that Marx believed in. However, Russia was really not developed enough economically for true communism to exist. The civil war that ravaged Russia after the revolution left the economy in ruins and the idealist leaders of the first revolution were eventually replaced or died, some in suspicious circumstances. Josef Stalin became the virtual dictator after Lenin's death and the state that should have 'withered away' became all-powerful. Stalin built up a personality cult around himself and any opposition, even from within the party, was dealt with ruthlessly. Although Stalin was a powerful dictator, he did not write a great deal, or formulate policies in the way that Lenin had done. The Soviet Union was ostensibly a Marxist-Leninist regime under his rule, although there was nothing like the society envisaged by either Marx or Lenin. Stalin believed in 'socialism in one country', which went against the internationalist ideals of Marxist-Leninist policy. This led to the Soviet Union becoming increasingly isolated economically. Stalin had to make Russia economically viable. To this end, he pushed through several disastrous policies, which were intended to bring the very backward peasant economy in line with the major capitalist nations.

COLLECTIVIZATION OF AGRICULTURE

Because agricultural production was inefficient, farmers were forced to join together in collectives and to work land in common. The state set the targets for production, set the price for the crops and bought up any surplus products. In theory, this should have worked, but in practice it failed because machinery and transport were inadequate. The farms were then inefficient. The state quota of the surplus product was set far too high so that peasants starved, animals starved and there was often not enough seed to sow for the next year. This is one indication of how difficult it is to put Marxist theory into practice, especially in a country which has not attained the level of development Marx believed would be attained before revolution took place.

FORCED INDUSTRIALIZATION

Stalin wanted to transform Russia from an agricultural society into an industrial one. He intended to do this by planning all industrial production from the centre. Production targets dominated political and economic life. Five-year plans were implemented, with set targets to be reached by the end of the allotted time. In industrial terms, the plans worked and the aims were achieved.

Russian industry developed rapidly, in ten years it was level with that of the capitalist countries who had taken nearly two centuries to reach the same level. In human terms, it led to great hardship for the people and a decrease in consumption, which eventually depressed the economy. Again this shows how difficult it is to put theory into practice, especially under the wrong conditions.

PURGES

Stalin wanted absolute power and the state became his tool. He used the army and the secret police to wipe out dissidents. Thousands were made to take part in show trials as enemies of the people and were sentenced to life in labour camps or mental hospitals. Stalin wanted to bring Russia into the modern world and was prepared to inflict suffering on the people in order to do it. It has been estimated that 20 million people died as a result of his reign of terror.

AFTER STALIN

Stalin ran the Soviet Union as a totalitarian state, and after his death in 1953 the leader who followed him, Nikita Khrushchev, denounced him as a dictator. Khrushchev wished to go back to the ideals of Marx and Lenin and this heightened differences with the regime in communist China (which until then had been one of their main allies), leading to a split between the two countries. The Soviet Union became even more isolated economically from the rest of the world and also politically as the **Cold War** began to take hold. The ultimate decline of communism in Russia is discussed later in this chapter.

Chinese communism

Russia remained the only communist country in the world until joined by China. Like Russia, China was not ready for revolution in the Marxist sense because it had a largely rural and illiterate population and little industrialization. In the 1920s it was ruled over by a warlord class in a feudal manner. Nationalist and communist groups formed a united front to try to overthrow this class but the alliance fell to pieces after interference from Stalin and Hitler.

After many years of fighting, the People's Liberation Army, under the leadership of Chairman Mao, declared the People's Republic of China in 1949. Mao was a brilliant military strategist and expert in guerrilla warfare. His victory, much like that of the Bolsheviks in Russia, was aided by another war that affected the internal conflict. When Japanese forces invaded China, in the Sino-Japanese war of 1937, many people joined with the communists in order to flee from the Japanese.

Chairman Mao wanted to educate the peasants into the ways of communism, so he wrote many texts loosely based on those of Marx. These became the basis of Chinese communism, also called **Maoism** or **Mao Zedong** thought, and were eventually published in the West as the infamous '**Little Red Book**'. This was sold very cheaply around the world during the 1960s.

Maoism is a further development of Marxist thought, and although it is officially still a part of Chinese communism in the twenty-first century, its influence has been greatly reduced since the death of Chairman Mao in 1976. Maoist thought differed from the traditional Marxist-Leninist policies and was much more militaristic. One of Mao's most famous sayings is that 'political power comes from the barrel of a gun'. He believed that class struggle continues throughout the socialist period that follows revolution, so that even after the proletariat seize power there is always the chance that the bourgeoisie will regain control. It was this that led to the formation of the Red Guard and to the **Cultural Revolution**.

At first Mao believed that rural development was the way forward for China and he ignored industrialization to a great extent until the Great Leap Forward, which began in 1957. This was an attempt to increase steel production and bring agriculture up to date. The Great Leap Forward, however, was not a success and its failure was largely due to inefficiency and terrible climate conditions. It led to terrible famine where millions of people died.

The Cultural Revolution began in 1966 and some see it as an attempt to divert attention away from past failures and focus attention on a scapegoat for the problems communism was facing in China. Mao stressed the importance of changing the whole mental outlook of society by transforming education, literature, art and any other parts of the superstructure that did not correspond to the socialist economic base. It was felt that the only true communists were the proletariat and anybody else was likely to be an 'imperialist'.

The Red Guard, composed mainly of students, was an all-powerful communist militia that imposed communist thought on the populace. Anyone considered to be an 'imperialist' was purged; intellectuals and anyone believed to have bourgeois thoughts were imprisoned, exiled to work in labour camps or re-educated; many disappeared. Traditional Chinese culture was ignored and followers of all religions were persecuted. The long-term result of this was that during that time, economic activity in China was virtually halted in favour of revolutionary activity, higher education was ignored and many young people were moved to rural areas to carry out propaganda missions. The effects of the Cultural Revolution are seen as disastrous, even among the communist party in China itself.

Since Mao's death, China has been gradually moving towards a free market economy under Deng Xiaping and has seen a huge increase in economic growth since the 1990s. China is still officially a communist state under an authoritarian single-party system, but many would say it is communist in name only. There is now a growing middle class, much free trade, and some indications that Confucian philosophy, which was previously banned, is becoming part of the culture again.

The Cold War

'A spectre is haunting Europe, the spectre of communism', Marx wrote in *The Communist Manifesto*. After the Second World War the spectre of communism seemed to be haunting the whole world.

This was the period of the Cold War when it seemed everyone was on the alert for 'reds under the bed'.

Insight

Fear of communism led to communist 'witch hunts' in the USA during the 1950s, led by senator Joseph McCarthy backed up by the FBI and The House Committee for un-American activities. Many Hollywood actors, writers and musicians were accused of being communists and blacklisted, persecuted or imprisoned.

The Cold War did not result in an actual military war with open hostility; it was a prolonged series of political, ideological and economic conflicts between communist and capitalist countries that lasted for about 45 years. It centred round a huge arms race involving nuclear and conventional weapons, largely between the superpowers of the USA and the USSR. It was feared that this would lead to a full-blown conflict, perhaps involving nuclear weapons, in which millions of people would be killed and the world totally destroyed. This was especially true during the Cuban missile crisis of 1962, which was the most openly confrontational incident in the Cold War.

Insight

The Cuban missile crisis came about when the US intelligence service discovered nuclear missiles had been placed on Cuba by the Soviet Union. There were some tense negotiations before they were finally removed and it was the closest that the Cold War came to an actual nuclear war.

In addition to the arms race, there was a huge propaganda war involving espionage and spy scandals and a kind of economic war with blockades and trade embargoes. Also, what have been called 'proxy wars' took place, where the superpowers became embroiled in the internal policies of overseas nations during civil wars, such as in Korea and Vietnam.

The origins of the Cold War are still being debated by historians. At the time it began, the justification for it was that Stalin's policies in the Soviet Union were expansionist and that as Marxist doctrine insisted on a worldwide proletarian revolution, then a conflict between capitalism and communism was inevitable. The way that the world was divided up after the Second World War played a great part in aligning the participants into 'blocs'. During the war, the allies – the United Kingdom and the USA – had been prepared to support communism in order to prevent the rise of world fascism. When fascism was defeated communism was seen as the main threat to the balance of power. The Soviet Union, as Russia was now called, and China were seen to be becoming more powerful. In 1947 President Truman of the USA made a declaration that the USA was prepared to counter communist expansion throughout the world. The US government was worried by the implications of more communist states arising not just as a result of revolution but also by the way in which the World War had been resolved:

▶ *Europe had been divided by peace treaty and many European countries came under communist control as part of the Soviet bloc. The Soviet Union was now one of the major powers and it influenced governments in states around it using military and economic aid. Berlin became divided by the Berlin Wall. An 'Iron Curtain' of secrecy was said to have come down between Eastern and Western Europe.*

▶ *There were fears that Communist China would come to dominate South East Asia. It was felt that 'the loss of Indo-China will cause the fall of South East Asia like a set of dominoes'. This was the **domino theory**, as described by President Eisenhower, and it led to USA involvement in Laos, Cambodia, North Korea and ultimately to the Vietnam War.*

▶ *There were revolutions in South America and Africa against colonial oppression. Many of the countries involved received aid from the Communist bloc in their struggle for independence. Communist governments in the developing world have included Cuba, Chile, Angola and Mozambique; all had differing colonial histories but received aid and arms from communist countries.*

Marxists have argued that the USA escalated the Cold War by the use of atomic weapons during the Second World War and that the nuclear threat was used as a way of expanding capitalism. Whatever the reasons for its origin, the Cold War was largely an imaginary war based on fear and mistrust that came from deep ideological differences between the communist and capitalist blocs. It came to an end in the 1980s, largely due to the decline of the communist economies in the Soviet Union and The People's Republic of China.

The decline of communism

The beginning of the twentieth century saw a rise in world communism, but by the end of the century it was in decline. At its peak, in the early 1980s, it was estimated that a third of the people of the world lived under some kind of communist government. Presently, there are only a few communist countries left; The People's Republic of China, Cuba, Laos, North Korea and Vietnam are the few remaining communist regimes under a single-party system. A large number of people still live under communist rule as the population of China is so vast, but the Soviet Union was dissolved in 1991 and many people regard this as the beginning of the end for communism and as proof that the ideas of Marx do not work.

Historians are still debating the causes of the break-up of the Soviet Union and many blame the arms race that came as a result of the Cold War. This was financially crippling for a country that was already economically and technologically backward and politically isolated. Whatever the reasons, the decline began in 1985 when Mikhail Gorbachev came to power and began to bring in the policies of glasnost (openness) and perestroika (restructuring). These were vital, as the country was virtually bankrupt and technologically very far behind the West. As it became more and more obvious that the Soviet Union was losing its power, many citizens of the satellite communist countries around its borders began relatively peaceful demonstrations against their governments. Eastern European Communist governments fell one after the other during the 1980s and in 1989 the Berlin Wall, once a great symbol of the Cold War, fell. Many of the republics within the Soviet Union began to agitate for independence and eventually there was an attempted coup against Gorbachev in the summer of 1991; following this, Boris Yeltsin became leader and the Soviet Union became a Commonwealth of Independent States. The Supreme Soviet, or the governing body, was dissolved in December 1991 and this is seen as the official ending of the Soviet Union.

Has Marxism failed?

Is the decline of the Soviet Union the beginning of the end for Marxism? Many people would argue that this is the case, but the response of many Marxists would be to say that the regime in the Soviet Union had very little to do with Marx except for the use of his name. They would describe it as a form of state capitalism, where bureaucrats acted as a form of bourgeoisie. The fall of the Soviet Union led to a great crisis of confidence in other communist countries that saw the Soviet government as a model for them to follow. They also lost trade markets and military support.

Critics would also point to the fact that China is now largely a free-market economy and not actually a communist state at all, and that the communist governments in Indo-China and in Cuba are reliant on Chinese economic support and so strictly speaking they cannot be described as communist either. Although officially North Korea (The Democratic People's Republic of Korea) is a socialist republic, it has been described as a dictatorship by its critics. There is some debate about the future of communism in Cuba after Fidel Castro's leadership ended. His age and ill health meant he passed the reins of government over to his younger brother in 2008. As personality cults are important in all communist states that developed out of peasant economies this change in leadership might affect the popularity of the communist government. There is much speculation as to how communism might develop in Cuba in the future.

Although it looks like the end for communism in many places, it has not stopped Marxists who are working towards power in the developing world, notably in India and Nepal. It is impossible to say what might happen in the future but this will be looked at in more detail in the final chapter.

THINGS TO REMEMBER

▶ *Marx died in 1883 but Engels continued to work on his manuscripts.*

▶ *His ideas were spread around the world through the labour movement and working men's groups.*

▶ *Marx wrote a vast body of work that has been interpreted in widely different ways.*

▶ *Russia became the first communist country in the world after a revolution in 1917.*

▶ *Communism developed in a way Marx would not have approved of in Russia and China.*

▶ *The Cold War was based on the fear of the spread of communism in the West.*

▶ *Communism failed in many countries because of economic problems.*

9

Marxism after Marx – the development of Marxist thought

In this chapter you will learn:
- *how Marxist theory was developed in the twentieth century*
- *about postmodernism and post-Marxist thought*
- *about the debate on Marx's relevance in the twenty-first century.*

There is no doubt that the ideas of Marx changed the world. Revolutions happened in his name and communist societies came into being. His ideas also led to a great deal of debate about the nature of society and of humankind, for he changed the way that we look at each other and at the world. In academic circles there has been continuing debate and discussion of his ideas for over a century. This has led to the splitting off of different schools of thought based on Marxist ideas, who develop them further. Since the fall of the Soviet Union, there has been less interest in his work academically; it has become 'unfashionable', especially as the academic world moves towards **postmodern** theory. However, with the rise of anti-capitalist and anti-globalization campaigns, including the eco-socialist movement, there are signs that there may be future developments in the aspects of Marx's work that look at the 'destructive' spread of capitalism and its relation to ecology.

This chapter aims to give some background understanding and structure to the many complex and conflicting theories that have been developed from the works of Marx. Some of these have been in favour academically and then gone out of favour again and some have always been controversial. However, it is important to have at least a basic understanding of them as many books on Marx assume knowledge of them.

There have also been numerous criticisms of his theories, especially as time has gone on. Many of his predictions do not seem to have come about and these will be discussed later in the chapter. In addition, there is also an examination of how relevant Marx is now that we live in a postmodern age.

Types of Marxism

Marx wrote a great deal and a great deal has been written about him, so that if someone claims to be a Marxist, the next question asked is often 'What kind?' As there have been numerous debates over who is the most accurate interpreter of what Marx wrote and many academic schools of Marxism exist, this is not an easy question to answer. There is also some confusion with the word **Marxian.** Marxian is often used by those academics who agree with a lot of Marx's methodology but not in the conclusions he reached, or in his predictions about the future of society. It is often used in relation to the study of political and economic systems. For example, Marxian economics embraces Marx's use of the terms 'means of production', 'surplus value', etc. However, those who use it do not necessarily believe the conclusions that Marx came to about alienation, exploitation and the need for revolution.

The main types of Marxism and schools of thought developed in response to his work are as follows:

CLASSICAL MARXISM

Classical Marxism is the theory of Marxism that Marx and Engels developed. It is based on what Marx said or wrote. Most of what has been written in this book so far would come under the heading of classical Marxism, including Marx's description of the capitalist society and historical materialism and the issues of class struggle, alienation, exploitation, revolution and communism. However, as Marx wrote a great body of work, there is still plenty of scope for people to disagree about what Marx meant by something or whether or not he might have changed his mind about it later. Added to this, is the fact that many Marxists have taken pieces of Marx out of context in order to prove political points.

Another problem in classical Marxism is that Marx changed his mind about some of the issues; sometimes he developed what he had already written and sometimes he refuted it, especially as his thought processes matured. Some Marxists would divide Marx's work into two broad categories of 'young Marx' and 'mature Marx'.

There is some disagreement about which works should be taken into account at each stage and where the dividing line is between his youthful and mature thought. It is observed that many of his earlier works are philosophical in nature as he was studying philosophy and still under the influence of Feuerbach. His later works deal more with economic theory and the materialist concept of history. This split is important to many Marxists because it seems to indicate a change towards a progressive kind of scientific socialism in his writing and this means that many of his earlier works could be said to be influenced by bourgeois philosophy and disregarded. In his book *State and Revolution,* published in 1917, Lenin claimed that *The Poverty of Philosophy* was the first work of the mature Marx. When The *Economic and Philosophical Manuscripts of 1844* were first published in 1932, they were seized on by those who wanted a humanistic explanation of Marx but they were suppressed in the Soviet Union.

Much of the more recent discussion of this division goes back to the works of Louis Althusser (1918–90), a **structural Marxist** who wrote a great deal on ideology and makes particular reference to the split between the young and mature Marx in his work *For Marx*, written in 1965. Althusser claimed that *The German Ideology* of 1845 marked the point where Marx broke away from his more humanist philosophical ideas and began a more scientific and materialist viewpoint. However, there have been others who disagree with him, such as Etienne Balibar, who wrote *The Philosophy of Marx* in 1991. These divisions between young and mature Marx do appear to be largely subjective and depend on what is trying to be proved at the time. Are the works of Marx a progression that develops through time and can we read the early works in isolation, knowing that the later works may contradict them? There are no conclusive answers in academic circles.

GRAMSCI AND HEGEMONY

One of the major thinkers who developed classical Marxism was Antonio Gramsci (1891–1937), an Italian communist. He was imprisoned by the Fascist regime in Italy in 1926 and began to write about what he saw as the failure of Marxist communism. Marx had predicted that a workers' revolution was inevitable, so why had the promised revolution not occurred? Gramsci agreed with Marx that there was a need for class struggle but he saw that many European workers turned towards fascism rather than communism and he wondered why this had occurred. Why was capitalism still deeply entrenched in the society around him? Gramsci's imprisonment lasted for eight years and during this time he thought and wrote intensively about these questions; over 30 notebooks and also thousands of pages on history and nationalism were later published as the *Prison Notebooks*.

Marx had written that the economic base was always the driving force of change; the superstructure of laws, culture and religion was subordinate to the economy. This is known as the theory of **economic determinism.** Marx had shown that the superstructure relied on ideology in order to instil a false consciousness about the economy.

Insight

As we have seen in earlier chapters Marx believed that each mode of production brings into existence its own unique ideology.

Gramsci agreed with this up to a point but thought that this view of society was too simplistic. He believed that the driving force in society was not the economy but lay in the dissemination of ideas that came out of the superstructure. Ideology was in fact an important and autonomous part of the class system, part of the total culture of society. Gramsci developed the idea of ideology much further, into the concept of **hegemony**. He believed that one class was still the 'dominant' class and in order to remain dominant it needed to have agreement in society that what it was doing was right and just and as it should be. The class needed to establish what he called 'spontaneous consent', so that there was no need for the ruling class to use force, or political or economic coercion to rule. All this class had to do was to make the workers believe in their perspective, through the means of religion, education and the media. In this way, a shared belief system becomes the basis for a form of class domination.

Gramsci did not believe that hegemony was a unified system of oppression forced on the workers from above, he saw it as a complex layered system that ran through society as a whole. People in society live their own life but are part of a small structure that is built up around them; they do not see how their life fits into the structure around them and how this slots into the structure of society as a whole. People assume that they have free will and autonomy, but according to Gramsci, a consensus culture had developed, where the values of the bourgeoisie had become the values of the majority of people in society. In some sense, there is a kind of mental or moral bargain made between the rulers and those who are ruled, which everyone accepts without thinking. It appears to be a natural and common sense view of the world but it is really the view of the dominant class. Although a minority of people may object to this view, they can be overcome by force if necessary, as long as the majority of the population are in agreement. Gramsci believed that all cultural institutions were suspect and all cultural practices and beliefs should be looked at critically and investigated for the part they might play in dominating society. Gramsci believed that the rise of fascism had come about because people were more concerned about buying into middle-class status and a consumer society than they were with working towards a revolution that would truly benefit them. The rhetoric of the fascist leaders, combined with the teachings of a bourgeois religious system, had blinded them to their true needs and made them believe that a culture of individuals in competition with each other was natural.

So, in Gramsci's view, the culture of a society is not a morally neutral system but is an expression of ideology, which is used to promote the views of the ruling class. The bourgeoisie were able to dominate the proletariat by manipulating social consciousness through religion, education and other cultural systems. Today we would include the mass media, such as television, radio, newspapers and web pages as part of the hegemony, for these are a more important part of the superstructure than they were in Gramsci's time.

Gramsci saw that the hegemony changed through time as circumstances changed, and that it was always possible for the proletariat to use the hegemony to their own advantage if they could get enough support from others in their society. It is possible to use hegemony to put forward an alternative view of the world; for example, communists could disseminate the idea that a revolution is desirable and possible. He saw that this would be easier to do in an unpopular dictatorship than in a social democracy where culture was very complex and relations between people and institutions are complicated. This is why he believed education was extremely important, for he also believed that anyone from any class could be an intellectual if they were given the chance to study and that it was important to establish a working class 'culture' to articulate the needs of the masses.

Gramsci was important because he saw that everyday culture was a place where political action could begin and he was one of the first Marxists to realize the power of the mass media. He was an influence on the thinkers of the **Frankfurt School** who developed Marxist thought at around the same time.

THE FRANKFURT SCHOOL

The Frankfurt School is a rather informal term used to describe a school of Marxist thought that evolved from studies into philosophy, social theory and social research at the Institute for Social Research in Frankfurt, Germany. The term refers to those who were actually affiliated to the Institute and those who were influenced by them, although they never used this term to describe themselves. The Frankfurt School was one of the early examples of what is sometimes called Western Marxism, in order to differentiate it from the use of Marxist thought developed in the Soviet Union and China.

The Frankfurt School began in the 1920s, but it became more important in 1930 when Max Horkheimer became the director of the institute and it became a focal point for dissident Marxists. They believed that many of the Marxists of their day were only parroting a narrow range of Marx's ideas in order to prove orthodox Marxist-Leninist ideas and ignoring many of Marx's original works and ideas.

They were greatly influenced by the fact that, although there had been a large socialist movement in Germany and much of Europe, the predicted communist revolution had not occurred and fascism had taken popular hold instead. They believed Marx had not been able to foresee the social conditions that were occurring and they drew on the works of other thinkers to fill in the gaps of Marx's thought. They were also influenced by the publication of Marx's *Economic and Philosophical Manuscripts*, which had only recently been published. The rise of the Nazis meant that many of the philosophers of The Frankfurt School were forced out of Germany in the 1930s and moved to New York, returning to Germany after the Second World War.

The Frankfurt School philosophers are well known for use of **critical theory**, as defined by Horkheimer in his 1937 essay *Traditional and Critical Theory*. In its original form, it was a social theory that went towards critiquing society as a whole in order to bring about desired changes and was a development on the Marxist idea of historical materialism. It attempted to integrate aspects of economics, social science, history, politics, anthropology and psychology. The Frankfurt School philosophers were interested in the role of ideology, hegemony and false consciousness in society and the way that the culture of capitalism perpetuated itself through the media. They were particularly interested in the role of language in this context. The study of media, art, film and other cultural systems from a Marxist perspective is often called **cultural Marxism**, and this aspect of the Frankfurt School's work influenced the thinkers of the Centre for Contemporary Cultural Studies based in Birmingham, who were influential in the 1960s and 70s.

The most well-known philosophers of the Frankfurt School who have written extensively on Marx are:

Max Horkheimer (1895–1973) who with **Theodor Adorno** (1903–69) wrote *The Dialectic of Enlightenment* in 1944. In this they put forward the idea that mass culture is used by capitalist society as a way of getting capitalist ideals into the unconscious minds of society. In this way the members of society become passive consumers and lose their individuality. Society becomes a homogenized mass.

Herbert Marcuse (1898–1979) wrote *Eros and Civilization* in 1955 in which he attempted to synthesize the ideas of Marx with those of Sigmund Freud, the father of psychoanalysis. He also wrote *One-Dimensional Man* in 1964. Marcuse believed that mass communication and consumerism had an insidious hold over the minds of people, which amounted to a form of totalitarianism. 'False needs' are set up by the consumer society through advertising and we are all then in the grip of an all-powerful consumer state that permeates our thoughts and turns us into cogs in the capitalist machine. Marcuse believed that by these means, the working class are sucked into the cycle of production and consumption, which works as an ideological force to blind them to the fact they are working to support the capitalist status quo. The title of the book comes from Marcuse's belief that thought becomes one-dimensional as critical thinking and opposition are leached away by consumerist society.

Jürgen Habermas (1929–) is a German philosopher who studied under Adorno and Horkheimer of the Frankfurt School in the 1950s. He later disagreed with many of the theories of the school, believing them to be too critical of modern culture, over-sceptical and pessimistic. His thinking is often called neo-Marxist and comes from the tradition of critical theory. He is mainly noted for his discussion of the idea that the public sphere of modern society does not allow a genuine democratic debate. This was first brought to the public view in his work *The Theory of Communicative Action* in 1981. Although critical of modern society, he is in disagreement with many postmodern thinkers who see the world in a fragmented way. This is discussed further in the section on postmodernism.

THE PRAXIS SCHOOL

This was a school of Marxist, humanist philosophy that began in Yugoslavia in the 1960s and began as an attempt to free Marxist thought from the narrow confines of Marxist-Leninist-Stalinist thought that was emphasized by the government of the time. The chief figures of this school of thought were Milan Kangrga, Gajo Petrović and Mihailo Marković, who published a Marxist journal *Praxis* in the 1960s and 70s. This became well known in international academic Marxist circles as a leading journal of Marxist theory.

They believed Leninism and Stalinism were not true to the original works of Marx and had been distorted for political purposes. They emphasized the works of the young Marx, where humanism was stressed and believed these to be the 'real' works of Marx. They were critical of existing communist regimes and were an influence on Western Marxism, stressing humanist aspects of Marx.

ANALYTICAL MARXISM

Also known as 'no bullshit' Marxism, this was a school of thought that came about as a result of George A. Cohen's book *Karl Marx's Theory of History: A Defence* in 1978. This took the unfashionable academic view that historical materialism is a valid system but looked at it in a new way, using techniques derived from **deconstruction**. Analytical Marxism was a popular school of thought in the 1980s and Cohen published two other books: *History, Labour and Freedom* in 1988 and *If You're an Egalitarian How Come You're So Rich?* in 2000. Analytical Marxism has largely disappeared as a school of thought in the twenty-first century although it still has some influence.

STRUCTURAL MARXISM

Structural Marxism is a description of the approach to Marxism put forward by French philosophy professor Louis Althusser (1918–90). He was very influential in the 1960s and 1970s, during a time of great political unrest in France. Althusser did not believe that there was such a thing as fixed human nature, or as Marx would put it, the 'species being', which could explain social change. In an extension of the ideas of Gramsci, he proposed that there are ideological structures in society which people comply with; but where he differs from Gramsci is that he believes these forces are not necessarily the tools of capitalism but have an autonomous material existence.

The concept of ideology and the related idea of hegemony have been largely rejected by postmodernist and post-Marxist thinkers as being too simplistic. They believe that in the postmodern world people are quite capable of seeing through media manipulation and of projecting their own interpretations onto media output. But what exactly is the postmodern world and how does it relate to Marx's philosophy?

POSTMODERN AND POST-MARXIST THOUGHT

Postmodernism is a term that is often used but is very difficult to explain simply; even those who are described as postmodernist thinkers cannot agree on exactly what the concept means.
The basic core of postmodern thought is that in an attempt to understand the complexities of the modern world:

▶ *it is sceptical*
▶ *it questions the ideas of absolute knowledge and absolute truth*
▶ *it sees the world as 'fractured'*
▶ *it relies heavily on the meaning of language.*

Many postmodern thinkers would argue that we live in a new kind of world in the twenty-first century. We have gone beyond the 'modernist' view of the world that developed out of the ideas of the enlightenment with its belief in rationality, objectivity and progress.

Insight

Modernism as a cultural movement came about after the Industrial Revolution when the ideas, traditions and rational certainty of the age of enlightenment were questioned, including art, architecture, literature and religious faith.

The rapid rise of new technology and the economic conditions of our age have meant that society has become decentralized and dominated by mass media. It has become a world that has gone beyond the modern and into the realm of the postmodern.

> **Insight**
> For a deeper understanding of postmodernist theory
> I recommend reading *Understand Post modernism*.

It is not possible to detail all the conflicting theories that surround postmodernism in this chapter, but I have summarized some of the main theories of the philosophers that are relevant to the way Marx and Marxism are perceived in the postmodern world:

Jacques Derrida (1930–2004) was a French literary critic and philosopher. His writings are notoriously difficult to understand and he is best known for his development of the idea of deconstruction: a blend of philosophy, linguistics and literary analysis. This questions the true meaning of texts and shows their inherent instability. He believed that language was a slippery and suspect medium that could never represent the 'truth' and that there is no form of truth in any kind of academic analysis, whether economic, political or philosophical. All interpretations and narratives have equal validity. In his book *Spectres of Marx*, published in 1994, he put forward the idea that Marx's ideas should be looked at as a moral system and not a scientific one.

Jean Baudrillard (1929–2007) was a French cultural theorist and philosopher. His early works were greatly influenced by Marx and were an extension of some of the basic Marxist theories. He agreed that the expansion of capitalism had brought about social change, but he believed that Marx had to be brought up to date to take into account the way consumer society was changing. He believed the world is a now a society of reproduction rather than production. This means that images and information are just as important to the economy as commodities; they have actually become commodities. Like Gramsci, he believed that the cultural superstructure has a power of its own and is not just a reflection of what happens in the economic base. He also believed that Marx's theories of the modes and relations of production do not take into account the rise of modern consumerism.

Jean-Francois Lyotard (1924–98) was a French philosopher and literary theorist who wrote *The Postmodern Condition: A Report* *on Knowledge* in 1979. In this he puts forward the idea that in the postmodern world nobody believes in grand narratives, or meta-narratives as they are sometimes known. Examples of grand narratives include large-scale theories or world philosophies, the view of history as a coherent progression, or the idea that science can know everything or can formulate a grand unified theory of everything. Marx's historical materialism and economic determinism are grand narratives and so, using Lyotard's perception of the postmodern world, people are less inclined to believe in Marx's philosophy and follow his ideas.

Gilles Deleuze (1925–95) and **Felix Guattari** (1930–92) wrote a book in 1972, *Anti-Oedipus: Capitalism and Schizophrenia*, in which they argued that capitalism represses individuals and gives them false 'mediated' desires which are connected to the production and consumption of goods; this is an extension of the beliefs of the Frankfurt School. Although they were Marxists, their views differed from the classical Marxist view, as they saw class as something of a myth, believing the working class to be a diverse mix of different types of people. They did not believe in a uniform working class that would join together to bring about revolution and saw the classical Marxist view of class as a false view. They believed that under classical Marxism women and ethnic minorities were often marginalized, and in their view class struggle is only one strand of a very complex social structure and not the basis of it. The Frankfurt School thinkers saw the state as a single monolithic entity and believed society had become a homogenous mass of passive consumers. Deleuze and Guattari disagreed with this point of view; for them, society was a diverse mixture of complex individuals and they saw that capitalism was becoming unstable because of its diversity. Their view of the self is a very postmodern one, in that they believe that is not necessary to be stuck with a single identity or fixed self, people have the choice of living out different 'lives' and reinventing themselves; they do not have to follow the social 'rules'.

Francis Fukuyama (1952–) is an American political scientist who put forward the idea that we have reached the 'end of history' in his book, published in 1992, *The End of History and the Last Man*. In this he proposes that liberal democracy, as practised in the United States and Britain, is the ultimate form of society, which in some ways seems very similar to the way that Hegel saw Prussian society in the nineteenth century. Fukuyama does not see our society as the final product of the 'universal mind'; he argues that Western civilization, based on liberal democratic values, fulfils humankind's needs in economic terms and satisfies our needs for self-esteem and recognition, that we are becoming 'actualised'. As we saw in Chapter 5, 'actualisation' is often used as a term to indicate the opposite of alienation; so in Fukuyama's view, living in modern Western society is not the alienating experience that Marx believed it to be. At the core of Fukuyama's theory is his belief that human nature is governed by a desire for recognition. He believed that there was no need for ideological struggle after the collapse of communism and the end of the Cold War. However, he has since written that scientific and technological changes may lead to developments in history, so it is not at an end after all. Critics of his theory would point out that although the Cold War has ended, there is no end to conflict between ideologies. There is talk of a new Cold War between Communist North Korea and the Western world and talk of a new nuclear arms race. At present, there are also numerous ongoing ideological clashes, including those between religious groups: Islamic, Jewish and Christian. These have been inflamed by terrorist acts and ideological conflict doesn't look like it's going away at present.

POST-MARXISM

Post-Marxism is a term used to describe those who have built theories on those of Marx but have gone further, so that they are outside or beyond what was considered to be Marxist thought. Post-Marxists have moved away from the economic determinism that is implicit in Marx's work and disagree with his concept of class, but they do believe that there should be solidarity between members of society. **Ernesto Laclau** (1939–) and **Chantal Mouffe** (1943–) became the best known of the post-Marxists after the publication of their book *Hegemony and Socialist Strategy: Towards a Radical Democratic Politics* in 1985. In this they analysed classical Marxism but from a postmodern perspective, drawing on theories of language and deconstruction from Derrida and also exploring Gramsci's theory of hegemony. They believe that social conflicts arise out of 'antagonisms' within the hegemony that are difficult to understand because of the complexity of society and the personality. Postmodern thought sees the individual as a series of narratives; for example, Laclau and Mouffe saw that a working-class person is never just a 'working class' person. They may be a single parent, from an ethnic minority, a woman and working class all at the same time. Each of these different facets of the personality may be in antagonism, or conflict, according to Laclau and Mouffe. Class is not a unifying structure at all. Everybody has a subjective view of society that depends on their experience; class identity is only a small part of this, so a class-based revolution is bound to fail. Conflicts will always be a part of society and it will always be unstable and changeable but people can group together, despite antagonisms, to take action at a local level.

Post-Marxists believe that the conventional democratic process actually alienates many people and they also believe that the state is always open to corruption, even under communism. They see a form of 'civil society' as the way forward, where people promote their own interests in the marketplace and achieve change by grouping together for local struggle.

Where does Marx fit in?

There is a great deal of argument over whether society has been pushed forward into a new postmodern age or if it is still part of the modernist world. Jürgen Habermas puts forward the idea that we are still living in the last age of the enlightenment, although some people would argue that even the postmodern world is over and we are living in the post-postmodern world. So how is all this relevant to Marx?

Marx was one of the first people to write about 'modernity' in a structured way, he documented the rise of technology and the effects of the Industrial Revolution. He also helped us to realize that society is not always as it seems. In this way he inspired many of the thinkers of the postmodern world, but their thought has gone beyond his and they have disagreed with some parts of his philosophy, especially his view that the history of the world is one of class struggle. There is a great deal of debate about the role of class in the world of today. Other groupings of people, along lines of ethnic identity, gender or age, for example, are seen as just as important as class. If there is no such thing as class, in the way that Marx described it, and no oppression by another class, what does that mean to the idea of working-class solidarity? Is there any way that revolution can come about when society seems to be made up of diverse fractured selves without any agreed values? Can the world be transformed by one belief system that attempts to find a solution to all the world's problems? Postmodern thinkers do not believe that there is a 'theory of everything'; Marxism is just one of numerous alternative ways of looking at the world – a subjective, grand narrative.

Radical Marxists, however, would not agree with this. They believe postmodernist theory is just another form of hegemony and an attempt to divert people away from the real problems that exist in the late capitalist world. They believe postmodernists are too busy celebrating popular culture and ignoring the fact that there are still many families living in poverty, even in the Western world, and this will not stop until the capitalist system has been overthrown.

Postmodernism can be seen as a form of cultural **relativism**, a philosophical belief that there are no universal or absolute truths. The only truths are relative to some frame of reference, in this case culture. This is seen as a problem by those who believe that you should fight against injustice, for how do you decide if something is unjust and how can you make moral or ethical judgements about anything? How far should people tolerate oppression and exploitation? Postmodernism does not have any answers to these questions. It does not even ask the questions.

Is Marxism relevant in the twenty-first century?

Many people see the collapse of communism as proof that Marx is not relevant to the world today. After the Soviet Union collapsed and the Berlin Wall came down, Communist China became more open to Western influence and its economy more open to free enterprise. People see the failure of communism as the failure of Marx, yet the communism that Marx envisaged has never existed.

What the history of the twentieth century shows us is the power of Marx's ideas to capture the imaginations of the poor and oppressed throughout the world. There is no doubt that his beliefs, or other people's, interpretations of them, changed the history of the world.

The relevance of Marx to today's society has been debated and discussed by many philosophers, economists, historians and other academics, as well as by fervent Marxists, students and drunken pub-philosophers. Almost everyone has an opinion on Marx, even if it is not a particularly informed one. There are three main arguments:

1 Marxism is not relevant today at all because it was never relevant. *His scientific method was flawed and his economic theory was completely mistaken.*
2 Marxism is not relevant today because it was a product of its time. *The capitalist society that existed at the time he was writing does not exist any more. There is no such thing as the proletariat now, so there will be no revolution. We are living in a postmodern world, which bears no resemblance to the nineteenth century. There is no such thing as class; huge theories of everything are false.*
3 Marxism is still relevant. *The failure of communism in some countries does not indicate that Marx was wrong. In fact he predicted there would be a swing away from his theories and that capitalism would try to fight back before it was finally defeated. The world may have changed but while the economy is a capitalist one, his theories are still relevant. Postmodern*

culture is part of the hegemony and an attempt to make people passive, interested in celebrity but not analysing anything.

The first theory is obviously wrong because even if Marx was totally mistaken about everything, many people have acted upon what he said, so it must have some relevance. There are still many millions of people living in communist countries, despite the fall of communism. Derrida wrote, in *Spectres of Marx*, that we can never be free of the past or our interpretations of it, so that Marxism is now a part of our consciousness. Even though Derrida did not agree with the historical materialism of Marxism, he saw that there was still injustice and poverty caused by economic oppression. Marx was the person who brought this to our attention and the problem hasn't gone away. The debate about the validity of Marx's methods does not solve anything.

The second and third theories can both be seen to be correct, to some extent, because of the sheer volume of work that Marx produced; it depends on which aspects of his work are being examined.

HISTORY

His 'scientific method' of studying history has been accused as not being scientific by modern standards. Karl Popper, a twentieth-century philosopher, believes that there is no real way of proving whether Marx's assertions are true or false as you could in a proper scientific study. However, Marx did amass and classify a great deal of evidence about past societies, and modern social science developed out of his techniques. He wrote and researched in a very structured way that attempted to use the scientific methods of his time, which were concerned with the classification of things.

ECONOMY

Marx was not a trained economist. Some of his predictions about the economy have proved to be false; for example, wages being pushed down to subsistence level. On the contrary, most people are better off in real terms than they were a hundred years ago. Other assertions have been correct. He predicted that large corporations would come to dominate world markets. At the end of the twentieth century, more and more companies merged into large conglomerates including banks, publishers and computer software companies. In the twenty-first century the trend continues with large supermarket chains taking each other over, buying up properties and forcing small shops out of business. Marx also predicted that industry would become more and more reliant on technology and that there would be periodic recessions – both of these predictions are correct.

Insight

The latest economic recession, that began in 2007, happened on a global scale and was partly attributed to a failure to regulate vast banking corporations.

CLASS AND SOCIETY

Society has changed for the better; in the Western world many inequalities have disappeared. Universal suffrage has changed the structure of society since Marx's time. In Britain we have free education up to university level and health services for all who need them, although many would see this as a two-tier system where the rich can afford to pay for better private treatment and education. However, it is still a great improvement on the Victorian era and the lives and health of most people in Britain are better as a result. The feudal House of Lords has been reformed, heredity is no longer the only criterion for belonging to this law-making body. Marxists would argue that the scandal over 'cash for honours' shows that merely reforming a law is not enough to change a political system.

Insight

The 'cash for honours' scandal that happened in the UK in 2006/7 is also known as the 'cash for peerages' scandal. It was alleged certain businessmen had given huge loans to the ruling Labour Party in return for being nominated as life peers by the prime minister.

Although the proletariat as Marx described it does not exist in the same way today, people still refer to themselves as 'wage slaves' and work hard to pay off debts to credit card companies. Debt is becoming a major problem in Britain as many people get caught up in the consumerist society. As Marx predicted, there is also still a huge underclass of the homeless and the unemployed.

PHILOSOPHY

Marx is much more relevant to today's world when we look at his philosophy. There are two main philosophical points to be considered:

1 *Human nature is not a fixed thing but alters with social and economic conditions. This means that society can be changed by altering the economic system. Nobody was aware of this before Marx brought it to our attention. However, the history of the twentieth century has shown that it is not as easy as Marx believed to create the society of equals that he thought could develop. The fact that communist states have been riddled with inequalities does not mean that Marx was entirely wrong, but perhaps he was more optimistic about the flexibility of human nature than most people.*

2 *The most important part of Marx's philosophy was the understanding he gave us about the nature of freedom. Under capitalism we appear to be free but because economic conditions control our work, religion, politics and ideas, we cannot control our lives or society. Depression is one of the top three causes of absence from work in the UK – could this be a sign of alienation? Of course, this is a supposition which is not easily proved, but according to surveys carried out by NOP in 2006 just 36 per cent of British people now feel 'very happy'; in 1957 the figure was 52 per cent. People are less happy than they were 50 years ago, despite an increase in material possessions. The fact that we even acknowledge the possibility of this alienation is because Marx introduced the idea. People are now much more aware*

of the social and economic influences which shape their lives and this is due, in part, to Marx who first brought it to our attention.

The future

The world has developed in ways that Marx could not have predicted in just 100 years. In the early 1980s, few people could foresee the phenomenal rise of the power of home computers, mobile phones, the internet; the extent to which technological advances would change aspects of our society in a short space of time. There are signs within the music industry and publishing that people are taking the means of production into their own hands; technology in the Western world means we can all record our own music and make our own books. This will affect the structure of society yet again in ways we cannot be sure of right now.

There is also a growing movement against globalization of industry and exploitation of workers in countries in the developing world. Capitalism has been accused of 'chasing poverty around the world'; as soon as workers in one country receive fair pay and rights then the products become too expensive, and so production is moved to another area of the world. At present in the UK, we are buying in many manufactured goods from China and Laos. This means that the proletariat exist outside our culture and society and become almost invisible. Many Marxists are a part of the campaign against globalization, which also includes religious and ecological groups. It is not clear how this will affect society in the long term.

To try to look at the development of Marxism over the next 100 years would be an exercise in science fiction. We cannot predict how technology will change our society. Perhaps work will cease to exist as a result of technological advances, perhaps society will be destroyed by some disaster and we will return to primitive communism.

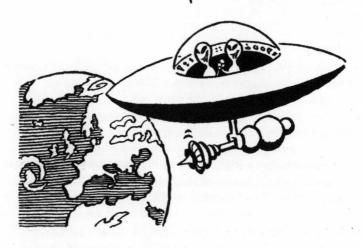

The revolution Marx predicted never took place, but does that mean it will never happen? Marxists would argue that as long as 10 per cent of the population hold 99 per cent of the wealth then there is no equality. There are still numerous Marxist groups in the world who believe that as long as society remains dominated by capitalism, there must be a revolution. As long as the ideas of Marx are still alive in the minds of people throughout the world, this must be a possibility.

THINGS TO REMEMBER

▶ *Numerous schools of Marxism flourished in the twentieth century.*

▶ *Marxism goes in and out of fashion in academic circles.*

▶ *Many people believe that Marx is out of date and not relevant to today's postmodern world.*

▶ *Others believe he is relevant because of the inequalities in society, and revolution could still occur.*

▶ *Marx's main contribution was to show us that human nature is not fixed and that even when people believe they are free, they are being controlled by outside influences of some kind.*

▶ *Society is changing rapidly in ways that Marx could never have predicted and technological advances mean that it is difficult to predict what may come next.*

Glossary

abstract social labour An economic feature of capitalism that treats labour as a commodity and separates it from everyday life.

accumulation of capital Where profit is not used to buy more products but is invested in future production.

alienation The feeling of being isolated or estranged from society.

anarchists Believers in the theory that society does not need government.

antithesis From ancient Greek, meaning negation. Antithesis is the second stage of Hegel's dialectic view of development, when the initial stage, or thesis, is contradicted.

Bolsheviks A branch of the revolutionary movement. Originally part of the All Russian Social Democratic Party.

bourgeoisie The middle classes who developed capitalism and took power from the aristocrats.

capital Money to which surplus value accrues.

capitalism An economic system where there is private property and relatively free markets where goods are sold for profit.

Chicago School An economic school based around Chicago University in the 1950s that advocated a laissez-faire attitude to economic systems.

Cold War Hostile measures between countries that just fall short of actual war.

colonialism The second stage of imperialism, where countries take over governing power.

commodity An object for use that is produced for sale.

communism A state where private property has been abolished, where people live in equality without classes or social divisions.

concrete labour This is applied to a product to give it value.

critical theory In Marxist terms it is a way of looking at the works and tradition of Marx and taking into account the varying criticisms that have been made of his methods and of Marxism itself.

cultural Marxism A form of Marxism that takes into account the role of the media, art and culture in analysis of society.

Cultural Revolution A revolution within Chinese communism that aimed to transform the superstructure.

deconstruction A method of reading texts based on the theories of Derrida. The idea is to look for inconsistencies and reveal the true meaning in what is written.

democracy A state governed by the wishes of the whole, adult population, where no smaller group has the right to rule. From the ancient Greek demos (people) and kratos (strength).

developing world Poor, less industrialized and under-developed countries, often former colonies.

dialectic The philosophic theory of contradiction and change.

dialectical materialism Marxist way of studying the relationship between the real world and the world of ideas.

dictatorship of the proletariat Unavoidable undemocratic state, made necessary after the Communist Revolution.

domino theory US theory of communist takeover and justification for interference in South East Asian politics.

economic base The way the economy is structured in society.

economic determinism The theory that the economic structure leads the development of society, politics and history.

economist A person who studies the science of the production and distribution of wealth.

economy The system by which wealth is created in society.

Engels, Friedrich Son of a wealthy textile manufacturer. He wrote about the plight of the working class and was a close friend of Marx.

evolutionary communism The belief that a communist state can come into existence through the natural disintegration of the capitalist system, without the need for revolution.

exchange-value The value that commodities have in relation to each other.

existentialist A philosophical movement based on the concept of an absurd or meaningless universe where human free will is an important factor.

exploitation Taking advantage of something or someone for one's own ends.

Fabian Society A socialist organization formed in 1884 that has links with the British Labour Party.

false consciousness False beliefs or values created by a culture or society.

fascism An authoritarian and militaristic political ideology.

fetishism Desiring, worshipping or giving excessive concern to inanimate objects; in Marxist terms this would be commodities, money or capital.

feudalism A system of land ownership that gave the nobility rights over the land, which they granted to their followers in return for services.

Frankfurt School A school of social theory that was set up in Frankfurt and was critical of orthodox Marxist thought as promoted within the Soviet Union.

French Revolution (1789–94) Revolution by the people against the French aristocracy. After a bloody uprising, the nobility were overthrown and replaced by a bourgeois democracy.

generalized commodity production Type of production under capitalism and free market economy where there is no regulation of who makes what.

Hegel, Georg German philosopher. His writings on the progress of civilization influenced Marx.

hegemony The subtle way in which the ruling class persuade the population to accept their view of the world as right and natural.

idealist philosopher One who believes there is a divine force of some kind that is responsible for the development of the ideas and beliefs of mankind.

ideology World view. The perception that people have of the world around them.

imperialism Economic and political domination of one society by another.

Industrial Revolution Term used by historians to describe the development of industry, and the factory system that began in Britain around 1750.

labour Work done to add value to raw materials.

labour power The strength and skill of the worker.

laissez-faire Unplanned and uncontrolled capitalism without any kind of government intervention.

Lenin Russian Communist leader. Inaugurated the dictatorship of the proletariat.

Little Red Book Popular name for The Thoughts of Chairman Mao. Millions of copies of this book with its distinctive red cover were distributed around the world.

manifesto A public statement of aims and policy.

Mao Zedong (Tse-tung) (1893–1976) Founder member of the Chinese Communist Party, he became head of state, or chairman, in 1949.

Maoism A type of communism invented by Mao Zedong in communist China.

Marxian Often used with reference to economics, this is a school of thought that believes that Marx's way of analysing the economy is valid and independent of the need for revolution or class change.

materialist philosopher One who believes all ideas and beliefs are a result of life in the material world, and not the result of intervention by a divine or supernatural force.

means of production Raw materials, factories and land, which allow production to take place.

nationalized Brought under state ownership.

philanthropy Practical benevolence.

philosopher A person who uses reason and argument to seek truth and knowledge.

postmodern A flexible term with many applications, literally meaning 'after the modern'. A way of looking at the world that takes into account the huge social changes that have happened due to technological advances, mass media and consumer society.

Praxis School A humanist school of Marxist thought founded in Yugoslavia.

primitive communism The type of classless society that existed in the distant past when people were hunter-gatherers.

productive forces A combination of the means of production, e.g. factories and machinery, with labour power.

proletariat The property-less working class in a capitalist system.

radical A person who wants fundamental change in a political system, usually through altering the basis of society.

Red Guard Communist militia, made up mostly of students, during the cultural revolution in China.

relativism The belief that knowledge and values are only relative rather than absolute. In other words, something can only be declared to be true in relation to something else.

revolution The overthrow of one ruling class by another, resulting in major changes to the structure of society.

revolutionary communism The belief that a communist state can only be created by a revolution.

slave society A society where much of the manual work is done by unpaid workers who do not have freedom.

social labour In feudal times this was labour done on behalf of society rather than for private enterprise.

social production A way of organizing work in society so that it is divided out fairly.

socialism In Marxist theory the stage between revolution and true communism.

sociology The study of society and social problems.

Soviets Regionally elected councils in communist Russia.

Stalin Russian peasant who became dictator.

structural Marxist A Marxist who follows a structural approach to Marxism as devised by Louis Althusser.

superstructure Cultural institutions which form a power structure within society.

surplus products Products over and above those which satisfy the basic needs of the producers.

syllogism A form of reasoning in which a conclusion is drawn from two given premises.

synthesis From ancient Greek, meaning union or amalgamation. The final, third stage of Hegel's dialectic, where the thesis and antithesis are combined.

terrorism The use of violence to make people accept radical social and political change.

theory of surplus value Marxist theory which explains how capitalists are able to profit from their workers' labour power.

thesis From ancient Greek, meaning affirmation. The first stage of Hegel's dialectic, where the original theory, or viewpoint, is proposed.

Tsar Russian emperor, or leader, of the semi-feudal society that existed before the Communist Revolution of 1917.

universal mind In Hegel's philosophy this is a rational spirit with purposes and ends of its own that lives through human beings, although it is not the same as the human spirit. Also known as Universal Spirit (translated from the German word *Geist*).

use-value The intrinsic value that a commodity has for its 'usefulness'.

Utopian Socialists Believers in a mythical perfect state.

vanguard of the proletariat Leaders of the communist
movement who aim to educate the proletariat.

Western Marxism A wide grouping of theoretical Marxists in
the Western world who do not agree with the interpretations
given to Marx in the Soviet Union and China.

Young Hegelians A group of radical thinkers who debated
the ideas of Hegel and Feuerbach. Marx was a prominent
member in his student days.

Taking it further

Timeline 1750–1917

Events in world history		Events in the life of Marx	
c.1750	Start of the Industrial Revolution in Britain.		
1775–83	American War of Independence.		
1789–94	French Revolution.		
1799–1815	Napoleonic Wars.	1818	Karl Marx born.
c.1830	Industrialization of Europe begins.	1835	Attends University of Bonn.
		1836	Attends University of Berlin.
		1841	Thesis accepted at University of Jena.
		1842	Works as a journalist.
		1843	Marries Jenny von Westphalen and moves to Paris. Becomes a communist.
		1845	Expelled from France and moves to Belgium.
1848	Riots in Paris, Vienna and parts of Germany and Italy.	1848	*The Communist Manifesto* published.
		1849	Banished from Germany. Moves to London.
			(Contd)

1851–2	Louis Napoleon declares Second French Republic.		
		1859	*Critique of Political Economy* published.
1861–5	American Civil War.	1864	International Working Men's Association founded.
		1867	First volume of *Das Kapital* published.
1870	Franco–German War		
1871	Paris commune proclaimed. Third French Republic established.		
		1881	Wife Jenny dies.
		1883	Karl Marx dies.
1905	First Russian Revolution.		
1914	First World War begins.		
1917	Bolshevik revolution leads to first ever Communist state in Russia.		

A summary of Marx's life

1818

Karl Heinrich Marx was born on 5 May at Trier in the Rhine province of Prussia, now Germany. His father was Heinrich Marx, a successful lawyer and his mother, born Henrietta Pressburg, was from Holland. Both of his parents were Jewish but before Karl was born his father was baptized as a Christian, probably as a result of anti-Semitism.

1830–5
Marx studied at the school in Trier and was assisted in his studies by Baron von Westphalen. He became acquainted with the Baron's beautiful and intelligent daughter, Jenny, who was four years older than himself.

1835
In October Marx began his studies at the University of Bonn, where he was supposed to follow courses on Greek and Roman Mythology and Art History but spent a lot of his time getting drunk and was involved in a duel.

1836
Heinrich Marx insisted that his son should move to Berlin University and devote himself to more serious study. He enrolled there in October for courses on Law and Philosophy. He became engaged to Jenny von Westphalen.

1836–9
Marx became a member of the Young Hegelians, a radical group influenced by the philosophy of Hegel but more materialist in their views. He was greatly influenced by Bruno Bauer, a lecturer in theology who was dismissed from his post in 1939 because he held atheist views. Marx neglected his studies again, this time because he became more actively involved in politics.

1841
Marx submitted his thesis to the University of Jena, on the advice of friends, who thought it was more likely to be accepted there than in Berlin. He was greatly influenced by the *Essence of Christianity*, which was published that year by Ludwig Feuerbach.

1842
In January he began writing for the *Rheinische Zeitung*, a radical paper, and by October he was made the editor. Under his

leadership, the paper greatly increased its circulation but it was closed down by the authorities for its criticism of the government and its coverage of social issues.

1843

In June he married Jenny, after a seven-year engagement. Her father approved of Marx but the rest of her family totally opposed the marriage. In the winter the couple moved to Paris, where Marx became a communist and began to associate himself more with working men's societies. He worked on the German-French *Annals*, a new paper set up by Arnold Ruge.

1844

The *Annals* closed down, but it was through their publication that Marx met Friedrich Engels, who became his lifelong friend. During this year he wrote the *Economic and Social Manuscripts*, although these were not published for another 100 years, and a *Contribution to the Critique of Hegel's Philosophy of Right.*

1845–7

Marx was expelled from France and in 1845 he and Jenny moved to Brussels in Belgium. He began to work more closely with Engels and together they wrote *The Holy Family*, a critique of Bruno Bauer and his followers, and *The German Ideology*. He also wrote his *Theses on Feuerbach*.

1847–8

He spent much of this year working on *The Communist Manifesto* with Engels. This was written on behalf of the Communist League, which had developed out of the League of the Just.

1848–9

Revolutions began in France, Italy and Austria. Marx moved back to Paris and then back to the Rhineland, where he started writing for the *Neue Rheinische Zeitung* in January 1849. He wrote several articles demanding that a constitutional monarchy should be set up in Prussia. These were seen as dangerous to the government and he was banished as an alien in May 1849. In August he moved to London and rejoined the Communist League, but he became dissatisfied with the London communists. He felt they were urging people to attempt a revolution before they were ready.

1850–64
Marx and his family spent these years living in poverty in two rooms in Soho. Engels supported the family financially, but did not have much to contribute until he became a partner in his father's company in 1864. Marx made most of his money writing articles for the *New York Tribune*, as its European correspondent. In 1859 his first book was published, *A Contribution to the Critique of Political Economy*. He spent much of his time researching in the British Museum Library for his greatest work *Das Kapital*.

1864–7
The International Working Men's Association was founded in 1864, and although Marx was not its leader, he was an important member and drew up the constitution. He attended meetings, several times a week, as a representative of the German council. In 1865 *Value, Price and Profit* was given as an address to a meeting in Brussels. He was also still spending a lot of time in his studies of economic and social history at the British Museum.

1867
Das Kapital, Volume 1, was eventually published after many years of work.

1868–70
These years were spent addressing meetings, working for the International Working Men's Association and working on the further volumes of *Das Kapital*.

1871
The Paris Commune was proclaimed in April. This was an assembly of left-wing politicians, workers and radical intellectuals set up after revolution. The Communards' rule degenerated into a reign of terror and was only defeated after a prolonged series of bloody battles. Marx

gave his support to the commune, believing it showed the way forward for communism; this led to arguments in the International Working Men's Association. Many members were moderate and wanted to gain workers' rights through co-operation with the government. They turned against Marx for being too radical. Another faction, led by Mikhail Bakunin, an anarchist, opposed him for not being radical enough. Marx didn't want to become embroiled in endless internal arguments; he felt these took him away from his studies. Eventually, the International moved to New York and disbanded in 1876.

1871–83

Marx became increasingly disillusioned by public life and became ill and depressed. He still continued to work on the next volumes of *Das Kapital*. His wife died in 1881 and his oldest daughter, Jenny, died in 1883. Marx himself died a few months later of lung disease. He was buried at Highgate cemetery in London. Engels inherited his papers and carried on with his work.

The writings of Karl Marx

Marx wrote numerous articles, essays and books in his life. These are the major works that contain his most important thoughts. Although many are not an easy read for the beginner, and not all of them are available from ordinary bookshops, anyone who wants to study Marx in more depth should read as many of his original works as possible.

- ▶ On the Jewish Question *(1844). An essay that is rather anti-Semitic but it sheds some light on Marx's view of the rights of man.*
- ▶ Contribution to the Critique of Hegel's Philosophy of Right *(1844). This was intended to be a full critique on Hegel's* Philosophy of Right *but the introduction was the only part to be completed. It is an important work because it is here that Marx first discusses the importance of the emancipation of the proletariat.*

- Economic and Philosophical Manuscripts of 1844 *(1844)*. *Also known as the* Paris Manuscripts. *These were not published until after Marx's death. The main theme of the manuscripts is the alienation that people suffer in a capitalist society.*
- The Holy Family *or a* Critique of Critical Critique *(1844). This was written with Engels as a criticism of the ideas of the Young Hegelians. The title is a sarcastic reference to the Bauer family. It was first published in Germany and not translated into English until after the deaths of Marx and Engels.*
- Theses on Feuerbach *(1845). These are short statements that Marx wrote to show how his materialist philosophy differed from that of Feuerbach. They were published by Engels in 1888. The eleventh thesis on Feuerbach is engraved on Marx's gravestone.*
- The German Ideology *(1845–6). This was not published until after his death and it was a collaboration with Engels. It is important because it states the theory of the materialist view of history and further discusses alienation in a capitalist world.*
- The Communist Manifesto *(1848). Written with Engels, for the Communist League, this is one of Marx's more important and well-known works. The first English translation was made in 1850. It was written as a direct appeal to the workers and so has the feel of propaganda. It describes the capitalist system and the creation of the classes of bourgeoisie and proletariat. It examines the idea of class conflict and calls the workers to revolution. It also gives some idea of how communism could be put into practice.*
- Wage-labour and Capital *(1849). This was produced from lectures given by Marx at German working men's clubs in Belgium in 1847. These were later published in* Neue Rheinische Zeitung *as a series that was never finished. Engels updated and revised the work before publishing his translation after Marx died. It explains Marx's economic theories including the growth of capitalism, how wages and profits are determined, and how this affects the worker.*
- The Eighteenth Bruimare of Louis Bonaparte *(1852). This was originally published in* Die Revolution, *a German language*

paper published in New York. The Eighteenth Bruimare refers to the date in the French revolutionary calendar on which Napoleon Bonaparte made himself dictator. In 1852 his nephew Louis Bonarparte proclaimed himself as Emperor Napoleon the Third. In this article Marx discusses French politics and history from 1848 until 1851, the date of the coup that brought Louis into power. The article is important because it explains his theories of the capitalist state.

▶ The Grundrisse (1857-8). These were notes made in preparation for A Contribution to the Critique of Political Economy and Das Kapital, and were not intended for publication. They were first published in Moscow in 1931-41 and were made available in translation in 1953. They are interesting to study because they show how Marx developed his ideas on economic philosophy and history.

▶ A Critique of Political Economy (1859). A short piece on economics that is important mainly for the preface, which summarizes the theory of historical materialism.

▶ Theories of Surplus Value (1861-3). These were contained in notebooks, and were not published until 1906-8. They are mainly notes for Das Kapital, dealing with the historical perspective of economic theory.

▶ Value, Price and Profit (1865). An address given to the First International Working Men's Association published after Marx's death. It explains most of Marx's economic theory in more simple terms than Das Kapital, including the theory of surplus value.

▶ Das Kapital, Volume 1 (1867). This is Marx's most important work, a long and detailed study of economics and its relation to history and society. It also gives evidence of the ways in which capitalists exploit workers.

▶ Critique of the Gotha Programme (1875). This was a commentary made on the document that was written during the Gotha conference, when two German socialist parties became united. Marx felt that the Gotha programme did not adhere to the precepts of scientific socialism. He wrote the critique in reply, and circulated it among German socialist leaders, but it did not have much effect on *the unification that took place. It was published after his death and is one of the few places where he discusses the ways in which a future communist society might be organized.*

▶ Das Kapital, Volume 2 *(1885)*. *This was published by Engels, and was based on notes that Marx left before he died. It gives more detail on economic theory but is rather dry. Unless you are an academic with a great interest in Marx's economics, it is probably not worth reading.*

▶ Das Kapital, Volume 3 *(1894)*. *This is another work published by Engels from notes made by Marx. It is slightly more interesting than Volume 2, but again it is of more use to academic scholars of economic history than to the beginner.*

Marx on ...

Some extracts from *The Communist Manifesto*.

COMMUNISM

A spectre is haunting Europe – the spectre of communism.

*

In this sense, the theory of the Communists may be summed up in the single sentence: abolition of private property.

*

Communism deprives no man of the power to appropriate the products of society; all that it does is to deprive him of the power to subjugate the labour of others by means of such appropriations.

*

In place of the old bourgeois society, with its classes and class antagonisms, we shall have an association in which the free development of each is the condition for the free development of all.

CLASS

The history of all hitherto existing society is the history of class struggles.

Freeman and slave, patrician and plebeian, lord and serf, guild-master and journeyman, in a word oppressor and oppressed stood in constant opposition to one another, carried on an uninterrupted, now hidden, now open fight, a fight that each time ended, either in a revolutionary reconstitution of society at large, or in the common ruin of the contending classes.

*

The modern bourgeois society that has sprouted from the ruins of feudal society has not done away with class antagonisms. It has but established new classes, new conditions of oppression, new forms of struggle in place of the old ones.

*

Society as a whole is splitting into two great camps, into two great classes directly facing each other – bourgeoisie and proletariat.

*

The ruling ideas of each age have ever been the ideas of its ruling class.

BOURGEOISIE

The bourgeoisie, wherever it has got the upper hand, has put an end to all feudal, patriarchal, idyllic relation. It has pitilessly torn asunder the motley feudal ties that bound man to his 'natural superiors', and has left no other nexus between man and man than naked self-interest, than callous 'cash payment'.

*

It has resolved personal worth into exchange value, and in place of the numberless indefeasible chartered freedoms, has set up that single unconscionable freedom – Free Trade. In one word, for exploitation, veiled by religious and political illusions, it has substituted naked shameless, direct, brutal exploitation.

*

Modern bourgeois society, with its relations of production, of exchange and of property, a society that has conjured up such gigantic means of production and exchange, is like the sorcerer who is no longer able to control the powers of the nether world whom he has called up by his spells.

*

It has been objected that upon the abolition of private property, all work will cease, and universal laziness will overtake us.

According to this, bourgeois society ought long ago to have gone to the dogs through sheer idleness.

*

The socialistic bourgeois want all the advantages of modern social conditions without the struggles and dangers necessarily resulting therefrom. They desire the existing state of society, minus its revolutionary and disintegrating elements. They wish for a bourgeois without a proletariat.

*

And here it becomes evident that the bourgeoisie is unfit any longer to be the ruling class in society, and to impose its conditions of existence upon society as an overriding law. It is unfit to rule because it is incompetent to assure an existence to its slave within his slavery, because it cannot help letting him sink into such a state, that it has to feed him, instead of being fed by him.

Society can no longer live under this bourgeoisie, in other words, its existence is no longer compatible with society.

PROLETARIAT

The proletariat, the modern working class, developed a class of labourers, who live only so long as they find work, and who find work only so long as their labour increases capital. These labourers, who must sell themselves piecemeal, are a commodity, like every other article of commerce.

*

The modern labourer, on the contrary, instead of rising with the process of industry, sinks deeper and deeper below the conditions of existence of his own class. He becomes a pauper, and pauperism develops more rapidly than population and wealth.

*

But with the development of industry, the proletariat not only increases in number; it becomes concentrated in greater masses, its strength grows and it feels that strength more.

*

This organisation of the proletarians into a class, and, consequently into a political party, is continually being upset again by the competition between the workers themselves. But it ever rises up again, stronger, firmer, mightier.

*

Of all the classes that stand face to face with the bourgeoisie today, the proletariat alone is the genuinely revolutionary class. The other classes decay and finally disappear in the face of Modern Industry; the proletariat is its special and essential product.

UTOPIAN SOCIALISTS

They reject all political, and especially all revolutionary action; they wish to attain their ends by peaceful means, necessarily doomed to failure, and by the force of example, to pave the way for the new social gospel.

Such fantastic pictures of future society, painted at a time when the proletariat is still in a very underdeveloped state and has but a fantastic conception of its own position, correspond with the first instinctive yearnings of that class for a general reconstruction of society.

INDUSTRIALIZATION

Steam and machinery revolutionised industrial production. The place of manufacture was taken by the giant, MODERN INDUSTRY.

*

Society suddenly finds itself put back into a state of momentary barbarism; it appears as if a famine, a universal war of devastation had cut off the supply of every means of subsistence industry and commerce seem to be destroyed. And why? Because there is too much civilisation, too much means of subsistence, too much industry, too much commerce.

*

Owing to the extensive use of machinery, and to the division of labour, the work of the proletarians has lost all individual character, and consequently, all charm for the workman. He becomes an appendage to the machine.

IMPERIALISM

The need of a constantly expanding market for its products chases the bourgeoisie over the entire surface of the globe. It must nestle everywhere, settle everywhere, establish connections everywhere.

*

It compels all nations, on pain of extinction, to adopt the bourgeois mode of production; it compels them to introduce what it calls civilisation into its midst, i.e., to become bourgeois themselves. In one word, it creates a world after its own image.

WOMEN

The less the skill and exertion of strength implied in manual labour, in other words, the more modern industry becomes developed, the more is the labour of men superseded by that of women. Differences of age and sex have no longer any distinctive social validity for the working class. All are instruments of labour, more or less expensive to use, according to their age and sex.

*

The bourgeois sees in his wife a mere instrument of production. He hears that the instruments of production are to be exploited in common, and, naturally can come to no other conclusion than the lot of being common will likewise fall to the woman.

He has not even a suspicion that the real point aimed at is to do away with the status of women as mere instruments of production.

*

Our bourgeois, not content with having wives and daughters of their proletarians at their disposal, not to speak of common prostitutes, take the greatest pleasure in seducing each others' wives.

Bourgeois marriage is in reality a system of wives in common ...

FAMILY

The bourgeoisie has torn away from the family its sentimental veil, and has reduced the family relation to a mere money relation.

*

By the action of modern industry, all the family ties among the proletariat are torn asunder, and their children are turned into simple articles of commerce and instruments of labour.

REVOLUTION

But not only has the bourgeoisie forged the weapons that bring death to itself; it has also called into existence the men who are to wield those weapons – the modern working class – the proletarians.

*

The immediate aim of the communists is the same as that of all other proletarian parties: formation of the proletariat into a class, overthrow of bourgeois supremacy, conquest of political power by the proletariat.

*

The communists disdain to conceal their views and aims. They openly declare that their ends can be attained only by the forcible overthrow of all existing social conditions. Let the ruling classes tremble at a communist revolution. The proletarians have nothing to lose but their chains. They have a world to win.

Working men of all countries unite!

Further reading

BOOKS

Works by Karl Marx
Penguin Classics have nine volumes of his works in paperback editions. These include all the major and more important works. The most important works for the beginner to read are *The Communist Manifesto* and *Das Kapital*, Volume 1.

Lawrence and Wishart began publishing the *Collected Works* of Marx and Engels in 1975. Eventually there will be 50 volumes, divided into four sections: Early philosophical works, General works, Economic works, and Letters. The major and more important works have already been published.

A selection of Marx's writings is available in *The Marx Engels Reader*, ed. Robert C. Tucker, W. W. Norton, 1978; *Karl Marx A Reader*, ed. Jon Elster, Cambridge University Press, 1986 and in *Karl Marx Selected Writings*, ed. David McLellan. Oxford University Press, 1977.

Works on Marx and Marxism

Berlin, Isaiah, *Karl Marx: His Life and Environment*, Fontana (1995). Originally published in 1939, this is a well-known, readable account of Marx.

Bottomore, T. (ed.), *The Dictionary of Marxist Thought*, Blackwell (1992).

Callanicos, Alex, *Against Postmodernism: A Marxist Critique*, Palgrave Macmillan (1990). Interesting look at postmodernism from a Marxist slant.

Cohen, G. *Karl Marx's Theory of History*, Princeton University Press (2001). A reprinted classic of modern Marxism.

Elster, Jon, *Making Sense of Marx*, Cambridge University Press (1985). A large systematic study.

Fine, Ben, and Saad-Filho, Alfrido, *Marx's Capital*, Pluto Press (2004). Marxian economics.

McLellan, David, *Karl Marx – his life and thought*, Macmillan (1973). A comprehensive guide.

Ollman, Bertell, *Alienation: Marx's Conception of Man in a Capitalist Society*, Cambridge University Press (1977). A readable account of the theory of alienation.

Stern, Geoffrey, *Communism: An illustrated history from 1848 to the present day*, C. Letts (1991). A summary of the way in which the ideas of Marx were spread around the world in the various forms of communism. It contains many fascinating maps and illustrations.

Wheen, Francis, *Karl Marx*, Fourth Estate (1999). A very readable account of Marx as a person.

Wood, Allen, *Karl Marx*, Routledge (2004). Philosophical views on Marx.

WEBSITES

Marxists Internet Archive
www.marxists.org
Probably the best online resource, containing nearly all of Marx's and Engels' writings, information and links.

Libertarian Communist
www.libcom.org
Has a very good library section.

Marxism Mailing List
www.marxmail.org
A moderated forum for activists and scholars. Also plenty of links.

In Defence Of Marxism
www.marxist.com
Website of International Marxist Tendency: discussion, calls to action and has some useful links.

Marxist.net
www.marxist.net
Website of Committee for a Workers' International. Useful links.

Victorian Web
www.victorianweb.org
Interesting resource showing the historical perspective of the times Marx lived in.

The Cold War International Archive
www.cwihp.org
Lots of original documents.

Index

Credits